CARTOONING CHINA

This book explores the series of cartoons of China and the Chinese that were published in the popular British satirical magazine *Punch* over a sixty-year period from 1841 to 1901.

Filled with political metaphors and racial stereotypes, these illustrations served as a powerful tool in both reflecting and shaping notions and attitudes towards China at a tumultuous time in Sino-British history. A close reading of both the visual and textual satires in *Punch* reveals how a section of British society visualised and negotiated with China as well as Britain's position in the global community. By contextualising *Punch*'s cartoons within the broader frameworks of British socio-cultural and political discourse, the author engages in a critical enquiry of popular culture and its engagements with race, geopolitical propaganda, and public consciousness.

With a wide array of illustrations, this book in the Global Perspectives in Comics Studies series will be an important resource for scholars and researchers of cultural studies, political history and Empire, Chinese studies, popular culture, Victoriana, as well as media studies. It will also be of interest to readers who want to learn more about *Punch*, its history, and Sino-British relations.

Amy Matthewson has a PhD degree in history from the School of Oriental and African Studies (SOAS), University of London, United Kingdom.

Global Perspectives in Comics Studies

Series editor: Harriet E.H. Earle, *Sheffield Hallam University, UK*

Global Perspectives in Comics Studies focuses on comics as an international form, with histories as rich and complex as the stories that fill the pages. We bring together original scholarship on a wide range of themes and theoretical concerns that span the globe. These texts present outstanding bold interventions into existing scholarly conversations, with the freedom (indeed, explicit encouragement) to collocate works by creators from different national and analytical traditions, as well as genres within the form. The books in the series are concerned with offering fresh perspectives on established concepts and theories through the comics form. Our aim in this series is to forge links across the field, to foreground artistic and academic contexts that are underrepresented, and to give attention to comics in all their various guises. Ultimately, this series wants to encourage readers to challenge their existing perspectives on a form that is central to the reading lives of so many.

Books in the series

Cartooning China
Punch, Power, & Politics in the Victorian Era
Amy Matthewson

Burning Down the House
Latin American Comics in the 21st Century
Edited by Laura Cristina Fernández, Amadeo Gandolfo and Pablo Turnes

Comics and Migration
Practices and Representation
Edited by Ralf Kauranen, Olli Löytty, Aura Nikkilä and Anna Vuorinne

For more information about this series, please visit: www.routledge.com/Global-Perspectives-in-Comics-Studies/book-series/GPCS

CARTOONING CHINA

Punch, Power, & Politics in the Victorian Era

Amy Matthewson

LONDON AND NEW YORK

Cover image: @ Getty Images

First published 2022
by Routledge
4 Park Square, Milton Park, Abingdon, Oxon OX14 4RN

and by Routledge
605 Third Avenue, New York, NY 10158

Routledge is an imprint of the Taylor & Francis Group, an informa business

British Library Cataloguing-in-Publication Data
A catalogue record for this book is available from the British Library

Library of Congress Cataloging-in-Publication Data
A catalog record has been requested for this book

ISBN: 978-0-367-45822-5 (hbk)
ISBN: 978-0-367-46099-0 (pbk)
ISBN: 978-1-003-02557-3 (ebk)

DOI: 10.4324/9781003025573

Typeset in Bembo
by Apex CoVantage, LLC

To: Helen Wang

CONTENTS

ILLUSTRATIONS

SERIES EDITOR'S PREFACE

I am delighted to present the first book in the *Global Perspectives in Comics Studies* series. *Cartooning China: Punch, Power, and Politics in the Victorian Era* is an incisive new study of the relationship between iconic British publication *Punch* and Sino-British politics in the Victorian period. *Punch* has been the topic of many research texts since the final issue's publication in 2002; these studies have tended to focus on the publication's position either as long-running serialised journalism or as a forum for satire.

Amy Matthewson pairs close visual analysis with historical contextualisation and research into the artists and publishers themselves to provide a rounded and comprehensive analysis of sixty years of *Punch* (1841–1901). Her dual focus on both the creatives and the specific political moment is both innovative and interdisciplinary. She deftly highlights the importance of considering the publication contexts and creators while analysing any specific theme. This book presents the ways in which political cartoons served as a powerful vehicle in shaping and disseminating constructions of China to a wider reading public. We peek behind the curtain into the world of the publisher and the often-turbulent connections between artists, their politics, and their personalities.

Matthewson's book has a broad interest base, given the inherently interdisciplinary focus of Comics Studies and the inclusion of Area Studies in her work. This means that this monograph would be of interest to scholars of comics (especially political comics and cartooning), journalism and serialisation, history, Chinese studies, politics, and sociology, with interest for those studying these subjects an additional market. Studies on political and editorial cartooning are not always fully welcomed under the umbrella of Comics Studies, despite there being clear arguments for their inclusion within the field. I hope that the publication of this study in an explicitly Comics Studies series will help lead to the inclusion of these subgenres in the wider academic conversation.

It is my great pleasure to introduce this book and to inaugurate a series that, I hope, will make a strong contribution to the development and internationalisation of Comics Studies.

Harriet E.H. Earle
Sheffield Hallam University
United Kingdom

ACKNOWLEDGEMENTS

Many people have been a tremendous support during the course of the research for this book. At last, I am able to acknowledge and thank those who helped bring this book to fruition.

My initial research began years ago while doing my master's degree at the University of Victoria. It was during this period of time that I had the great pleasure of being supervised by Gregory Blue, who continues to inspire and support me on my research endeavours. I am thankful for his inexhaustible patience and invaluable comments over the years.

I would like to thank my doctoral supervisors at the School of Oriental and African Studies, University of London, Lars Laamann, and Andrea Janku for their invaluable insights and guidance. My thanks go to Frances Wood for her support and to Lily Chang for her limitless patience and constant encouragement.

Thank you Harriet Earle, my editor, for your enthusiasm right from the start. I am grateful to Shoma Choudhury and Shloka Chauhan, who have been responsive and patient throughout the process. Thank you Helen Walasek for always being interested and excited about this research.

The research for this book would not have been possible without the generosity from institutions, for which I am grateful. SOAS, University of London for the Research Studentship, Language Acquisition Support, and Travel Grants; Universities' China Committee in London; the Sino-British Fellowship Trust, and the British Association for Victorian Studies.

With affection, this book is dedicated to my extended family. Thank you for all the support, love, and laughter. Arjmand Aziz, Lois Barnett, Olena Borodyna, Nancy Charley, Joy Fisher, Gary and Trudy Hamilton, Eric "Ba" Haaranen, Irene González-López, Laura Misic and Leo Misic, Yen Ooi, Sofia Podlegaeva, Josepha Richard, Margaret Scaia, Anita Siu, Marcia Thompson, Kevin Thompson, Janice Tsai, and Monica Walker; to the Brunch Ladies: Angela Cheung and Laurie Taylor; to the Confabulists: Paul Bevan, John Cloake, Mary Ginsberg, Helen Wang; to the Cultured Ladies: Flore Janssen and Eleanor Veness.

1

INTRODUCTION

On 4 July 1900, *Punch* artist Edward Linley Sambourne created a Chinese Humpty Dumpty on the cusp of a great fall (Figure 1.1). The image is captivating with all its meaningful details found within this seemingly simple image. The caricature depicts exaggerated features to denote racial difference, the style of clothes and hair braided into a queue highlights foreignness, and the archaic sword and animalistic hands represent barbarity. By situating this cartoon within the broader historical and epistemological contexts, the Chinese Humpty Dumpty offers cultural codes *Punch* readers could understand: a familiar and well-loved nursery rhyme used to convey patriotism and imperialist ideology. The image directs the viewer to gaze upon a Chinese Humpty Dumpty just about to take his tumble at a time when Britain and China were engaged in armed conflict during the Boxer Uprising. The perspective is from a British soldier among, perhaps holding, one of the modern bayonets in the foreground of the image. The cartoon laughs away the feasibility of a victorious China, dispelling anxieties of any upset to the racial hierarchical order or Britain's position on the international stage. For, as the nursery rhyme tells us, when Humpty Dumpty tumbles off of the Great Wall, all the Emperor's horses, and all the Emperor's men, will not be able to put Humpty together again.

This book explores the series of cartoons alongside the textual satires of China and the Chinese that were created in the British satirical magazine, *Punch*, since its founding in 1841 until the death of Queen Victoria in 1901, thereby bringing an end to the Victorian period. The examination of this popular magazine reveals a nuanced understanding into how *Punch* used China as a site upon which wider anxieties of Britain's social stratifications, as well as its global position as an imperial power, were both shaped and negotiated. I begin with the image of the Chinese Humpty Dumpty because it offers a fascinating conflation of visual imagination and the power of cartoons and caricatures in disseminating a particular set of ideas about China. The visual and textual satires were, in fact, not about

DOI: 10.4324/9781003025573-1

FIGURE 1.1 "Untitled" *Punch*, Vol. 119 (4 July 1900), p. 1.

Source: Punch, or The London Charivari

China at all; rather, they reveal Britain's knowledge of China – or what British readers thought they knew – the continually evolving Sino-British relationship, and fluctuating anxieties and tensions at different stages of Britain's imperialist developments.

As perceptions of China changed, so too did the visual and textual discourses circulating in British society, including those transmitted into satirical form in the pages of *Punch*. The setting and tone of *Punch*'s representations of China ebbed and flowed along with events and circumstances and formed an important part of a broader visualisation and discourse of China within Victorian society. These cartoons offer a complex understanding of the various, and at times contradictory, forms of China within the British imaginaries which, in turn, reveal British self-perceptions and self-reflexivity on its own society as well as its role in the world at large.

While there were other prominent newspapers and magazines, *Punch* wielded considerable cultural and political influence in British society, in particular among the middle class. *Punch* did not, however, reflect "Victorian society" as a collective entity. John Ruskin was right when he highlighted that the visual world that *Punch* satirised was exclusively London. He remarked that three of *Punch*'s artists, John Tenniel, John Leech, and George du Maurier, are "in the most narrow sense, London citizens . . . the street-corner is the face of the whole earth, and the only two quarters of the heavenly horizon are the east and west – End."[1] In the words of Dominic Williams, *Punch* is a useful source because "it offered a particular class an image of itself, its nation, and its place in the world."[2]

The aim of this book is to place political cartoons and caricatures front and centre of serious historical enquiry in order to explore the complex networks of ideas, attitudes, and ideologies of a particular class in Victorian society. *Punch* provides an excellent case study as the magazine's cartoons were significant conveyors of information and powerful agents that shaped perceptions of the self and "other" in nineteenth-century Britain. Political cartoons point to the complexities in the relationships between artist, writers, editors, the processes by which they were made for an intended audience as well as the socio-political frameworks in which they arose. Due to their ephemeral nature, they are invaluable sources in attempting to understand past attitudes; while cartoons do not passively reflect reality, they do "help to crystallise attitudes, and express in pithy and succinct fashion the thinking of a broad segment of society."[3] *Punch*'s series of cartoons of China highlight the unequivocal power dynamics in Victorian Britain's social and racial hierarchies during a time of social tensions and imperial fervour at home as well as geopolitical awareness and heightened consciousness of Britain's standing on the international stage.

Theoretical framework

On representation

As early as 1814, official records make reference to the Chinese as transient seamen employed by the East India Company but their numbers were minimal and apart from intermittent visitors and diplomats, the first Chinese did not appear in Britain with frequency until the treaties of Nanking and Peking in 1842 and 1860, respectively.[4] By the 1890s, the China-born population of the metropole amounted to approximately three hundred.[5] This negligible number is important when considering the ways in which "knowledge" circulated about an essentially invisible and voiceless community. During a time of frequent Sino-British contact and clashes, information about China and its people was disseminated through a range of text, such as traveller accounts and news media, as well as visuals, such as exhibitions, illustrated periodicals, and personal photographs that were taken by travellers and the foreign community in China and then sent home to family and friends in Britain.

The act of making something or someone visible is to gain knowledge and power, however, illusive. *Punch* did not create new visions of the Chinese; rather, they used familiar tropes to provide its readers with a sense of reassurance and stability in an ever-changing and uncertain world of imperialism, global capitalism, and immigration. These caricatures signified a way to classify and understand thereby rendering people, places, and objects less frightening and threatening. As Richard Scully and Andrekos Varnava point out, comic artists "can give singular form to the multiple, more nebulous conceptions on which they draw for inspirations, then disseminate those images to mass readerships."[6] As convenient visual stereotypes, the Chinese became "recognized, normalized, and therefore incorporated into established power relations."[7] The link between power and visibility is significant and will be further expanded upon in two key themes: the first is power behind representation (in this case, *Punch* magazine) and the second is power of representation (the images themselves as cartoons and caricatures).

Power behind representation

Who has the authority and power to represent and who is being represented? In Edward Said's 1978 work, *Orientalism*, he argues that in the post-Enlightenment period, Europe held the power to represent, manage, and even produce the societies and peoples of Asia, Africa, and the Middle East "politically, sociologically, militarily, ideologically, scientifically, and imaginatively."[8] By focusing primarily on nineteenth- and twentieth-century Western scholarship of the Islamic world, Said suggested that Oriental studies presumed differences to be ontological and this "imaginative historical discourse" was both disseminated and maintained through various hegemonic institutions.[9] While Said's work quite rightly underscores the correlation between the production of knowledge and dynamics of power, he does not refer specifically to the history between Europe and China, a complex relationship that moves beyond his theory that places the former in a superior position. The nuanced theoretical argument of Homi Bhabha on the ambivalence of colonial stereotypes better illustrates *Punch*'s series of textual and visual satires of China and the Chinese.

The power of the colonial stereotype, Bhabha argues, is in the process of ambivalence. For it is this force that

> gives the colonial stereotypes its currency: ensures its repeatability in changing historical and discursive conjunctures; informs its strategies of individuation and marginalization; produces that effect of probabilistic truth and predictability which, for the stereotype, must always be in *excess* of what can be empirically proved or logically construed.[10]

Colonial discourse demands an array of differences, racial, cultural, and historical, in order to enable "political practices of racial and cultural hierarchization" but this otherness is also both desirable and repulsive. The stereotyped subject is simultaneously unknown and familiar, "other" and yet fully known and knowable thus occupying an in-between space of ambivalence.[11] Bhabha argues that only by removing binary structures and acknowledging the dynamics of ambivalence can the cycle of repetition in colonial discourse be broken.[12]

British notions and attitudes of China, as Bhabha states, fluctuated between extremes of adulation and derision. The creation and dissemination of Chinese stereotyped figures "undercut their ability to represent themselves"[13] and *Punch* members of staff "devoted much time and talent to mocking or laughing at people far beyond their own class and ethnicity – namely, the Other."[14] With all these important considerations in mind, how does one

> *represent* other cultures? What is *another* culture? Is the notion of a distinct culture (or race, or religion, or civilization) a useful one, or does it always

get involved either in self-congratulation (when one discusses one's own) or hostility and aggression (when one discusses the "other")?[15]

The points of oscillation between admiration and contempt within the series of *Punch* cartoons of China coincided with imperial rivalries within changing socio-political circumstances. The subjects were chosen on the basis of topicality in the daily press and thus the news media was integral in circulating ideas and solidifying attitudes.

By the late nineteenth and early twentieth centuries, the media was already understood as an adjudicator able to sway public opinion, and questions arose on the function and power of the press. The Liberals, such as John A. Hobson, believed that the press functioned as a commercial enterprise that tended to cater to the most popular and, regrettably, lowest taste, in order to appeal to the widest audience needed to attract advertisers. Others believed the press was an opportunity to make positive changes in society.[16] This commercialisation and manipulation of the press captured the interest of the German philosopher Jürgen Habermas. His research originally published in 1962 titled *The Structural Transformation of the Public Sphere* calls attention to *die Öffentlichkeit*, the public sphere. His work explores the shift in function of the public sphere, which, he argues, moved from a space of rational and critical debate to the current system of "refeudalization" in which large organisations manage, exploit, and propagate public opinion.

Originating in the eighteenth century, the public sphere offered private individuals a space to debate public matters and this gave citizens the ability to influence power by forming a consensus and holding the state accountable. Habermas pinpoints a dramatic change by the second half of the nineteenth century when the press underwent a transformation in its development and commercialisation, resulting in the media shaping debates and opinions rather than being a vehicle of transmission. He points to "opinion management" that not only resides in advertising but also extends to "creating news events or exploiting events that attract attention." The press thus manipulates public opinion by employing "psychology and techniques of the feature and pictorial publicity connected with the mass media and with their well tested human interest topics."[17]

Habermas' argument is compelling, however, scholars have been quick to point out that he idealises the bourgeois public sphere. Habermas neglects the plebeian public sphere, thereby ignoring the varied institutions, such as trade unions and their corresponding value systems. There is also an absence of minority groups and gender in his discussion. Nevertheless, his theory is both useful and applicable in relation to this study. *Punch* staff members were all white men from the bourgeoisie and thus the composition of the magazine excluded the voices of the working class, minority groups, and women. Habermas' arguments on the problems of representation in the media, the relationship between the media and politics, and the media's ability to manipulate public opinion are especially relevant, as will be made clear in the following chapters.

An essential aspect that Habermas fails to discuss is visual forms of communication. He deals with rational and critical argument as a verbal process and only includes visual language when he refers to the ways in which the press manipulates public opinion. Is it feasible to have a rational debate through visual argument? I cannot provide an answer to this but am intrigued by the possibility. *Punch* artist Charles Keene found it easier to illustrate his meaning in conversation than to explain it in words. George Layard records dinner one evening when Keene, noticing the lady next to him confused about something he said, decidedly took the menu-card to sketch out his explanation. "I'll draw it, then you'll see," he tells her.[18] John Berger argues that art reproductions are not simply illustrations but they are themselves arguments. They argue about the original and thereby create a new language of images. What really matters about this visual language is, as Berger asserts, "who uses that language for what purpose."[19]

Victor S. Navasky puts forward the idea of the utilisation of visuals in critical argument, questioning the possibility while considering that the meaning in images is in a constant state of fluidity and cannot be controlled once released. Visual argument is therefore open to uncertainty and misunderstanding while simultaneously, and paradoxically, able to fix meaning or an idea into one's head. Most frustrating for the target of satirical attack, there is little recourse to defend oneself. Navasky explains,

> if you don't like something that is written about you, you can always send a letter to the editor, even if only in your head. The wounding caricature does not easily lend itself to such a remedy. And because an image is more "public" than words . . . it can be more humiliating . . . and its target may feel unfairly victimized and impotent to do anything about it. The only way really to answer a cartoon is with another cartoon, and there is, for all practical purposes, no such thing as a cartoon to the editor.[20]

For Navasky, one of the most significant aspects of cartoons and caricatures is that they are visual and thus more powerful than words. Keene would have agreed. He sometimes complained that his *Punch* cartoons failed to be appreciated because of the accompanying captions. Layard mused that by comparison to the image Keene created, the text seemed "like the sermon to the deaf Suffolk woman" and was "won'erful poor stuff."[21]

For *Punch* readers, it was easy to skim through or entirely dismiss the columns of text, but not the cartoons. *Punch* artist and writer William Thackeray was right when he annoyed his writer colleagues by commenting that most people bought the magazine for its pictures.[22] To Henry James, "social and political caricatures . . . [are] only journalism made doubly vivid" and while journalism "provides the criticism of the moment *at* the moment," it is a caricature that provides "criticism at once simplified and intensified by a plastic form."[23] The following section takes a closer look at the power of cartoons and caricatures in what Habermas calls "dramatic presentation of facts and calculated stereotypes" in order to reorient "public opinion by the formation of new authorities or symbols which will have acceptance."[24]

Power of representation

Caricature, from the Italian *caricare* meaning "to load," refers to figures with exaggerated and/or distorted features in order to produce a comedic effect and they reside within a cartoon which provides the setting.[25] Since at least the eighteenth century, caricatures have been relegated to the status of "low'" art and condemned for violations against the canons of beauty and in this way, satirical prints were both notable and distinguishable from "high" art. The use and location of satirical prints also differentiate them from other forms of art. Paintings, for example, have a prominent place in the home or in institutions and are dictated by rules of decorum and status whereas prints are much more easily made and transported.[26] During the nineteenth century, prints of political cartoons commenting on current events could be rapidly circulated among friends and family while those events were still making headlines in newspapers and at the forefront of people's consciousness.[27]

One of the remarkable skills of cartoonists is the ability to illustrate their target in "three or four strokes"[28] while retaining the "essence" of the person or thing being satirised. The aim is to enable viewers to immediately recognise who or what is being ridiculed by a few simple exaggerations or recurring fixed details. Lord Palmerston's caricature, for example, was remarkably precise, and he was immediately recognised in Wales by a mail carrier who saw his caricature in *Punch*. Other figures were not as easy to illustrate. Richard Cobden caused much dismay among the *Punch* artists as he had "a most difficult face to sketch, and *Punch* was in despair at the impossibility of producing a caricature that could be recognised without explanatory text."[29] The simplification in reducing people to their essence is significant; this skill, combined with exaggerated features, converts caricatures into supercharged images.

The Swiss comic artist, Rodolphe Töpffer explains, "what reminds us instantly, completely, is much less what resembles the object as what resembles *our idea of the object*."[30] He gives the example of an outline of a donkey with "four fine legs, an ample belly, a thin tail, and two long ears"[31] asserting that an observer will immediately recognise the contour as belonging to a donkey even if it is in no way the actual animal. The emergence of viewers' idea of what constitutes a donkey is therefore rapidly awakened with only a few simple lines that capture the essential elements. This pared-down approach eliminates superficial glamour or traits best kept hidden from public view and conjure up the essence of what or who is being depicted, effectively forcing viewers to focus on what could easily be missed. The best cartoonists are said to be highly skilled at manipulating physiognomy for the purposes of exposing "the sometimes ugly truth beneath the surface of those lines."[32]

Caricatures have the power to portray public figures in such a ludicrous or unflattering light that their reputation can be damaged or destroyed. It was the Victorians who first fully understood cartoons and caricatures as an influential art form that wielded power to shape and persuade public opinion through mockery.[33] The British politician A.J. Mundella declared "*Punch* is almost the most dangerous antagonist that a politician could have opposed to him – for myself I would rather have *Punch* at my back in any political or social undertaking than half the politicians of the House of Commons."[34] Benjamin Disraeli made an effort to curry favour with *Punch* artist John Leech in the 1840s while Disraeli's arch-rival William Gladstone accepted with pleasure an invitation to dine at the *Punch* Table in 1893.[35] Across the Atlantic, Boss Tweed, the nineteenth century New York State Senator, expressed outrage at the effects that caricatures of himself had on public opinion when he exclaimed, "I don't care what they print about me, most of my constituents can't read anyways – but *them damn pictures*!"[36]

These politicians were acutely aware that one effective cartoon could seriously damage their reputation, despite the seemingly harmless nature of the image. The seriousness of satire is an important distinction between it and comedy, a separation made apparent in newspapers where political cartoons are always found in a different section, away from the daily funnies. Satire tends to offer biting critiques and opinions to current social and political events, while the aim of comedy is solely to elicit laughter and tends to be dismissed as entirely lacking in seriousness. E.B. White explains, "the world likes humor, but it treats it patronizingly. . . . It feels that if a thing is funny it can be presumed to be something less than great, because if it were truly great it would be wholly serious."[37] This does not mean that satire is only didactical and not amusing; *Punch* artist John Tenniel declared, "I believe that I have a very keen sense of humour, and that my drawings are sometimes really funny!"[38] Indeed, it is precisely the outwardly light-hearted humour of satirical cartoons that is deceptive because within the joke, lay a cutting critique. As Mark Twain famously observed, "against the assault of laughter, nothing can stand."[39]

Political cartoons have thus been lauded as upholders of democracy and freedom of expression as well as effective tools in challenging or subverting established systems. In *The New York Review of Books*, Ronald Dworkin wrote that cartoons "and other forms of ridicule have for centuries, even when illegal, been among the most important weapons of both noble and wicked political movements."[40] The right to ridicule, however, is a double-edged sword; twenty-first-century cartoon controversies such as the *Jyllands-Posten* "Muhammad" caricatures (2005), the *Charlie Hebdo* massacre (2015), and most recently, the *Herald Sun*'s Serena Williams caricature (2018), have brought into focus the ways in which political cartoons can support and maintain inequalities. At times, cartoons have had a negative effect upon minority communities when the cartoonists employ exaggerated stereotypes that revive and perpetuate racist visualities.[41]

At first glance, a caricature can appear to be "so shot through with explanation," such an obvious propagation of ideology or so typical and familiar in its stereotypes that it removes the need for critical enquiry, but in reality, these illustrations give visual shape to current socio-political events and help to define a particular attitude.[42] In an increasingly globalised world, cartoons engaging with gender, class, race, or religious sensitivities need to be carefully considered and approached with due care. Steve Bell contends that cartoonists "have a remarkable opportunity to get through to people in a direct way [because people] read [cartoons] in a second."[43] W.J.T. Mitchell reminds us that pictures have a life of their own and thereby cannot be controlled once they are out for public viewing as meaning changes according to the observer. The message could also be confused or misunderstood as viewers try to "read between the lines" and, in this way, may be trying to "learn something that the artists did not know they were teaching."[44] *Punch* artists were highly conscious of the importance in making the message behind their cartoons understood and one of the ways in which this was achieved was through the use of visual metaphors.

Visual metaphors are essential to translate abstract concepts or complex structures into an easily comprehensible image. The use of metaphors is, however, contradictory; on the one hand, they are employed as a strategy to simplify complicated ideas and on the other, they challenge the mind to question the relevance, reality, and truth of the subject because metaphors proclaim to be true when in reality, like Töpffer's donkey, they are not. The formation of lines does not equate to an actual donkey and this tension needs to be decoded by the viewer. Rudolf Wagner argues that decoding metaphors is processed by viewers' familiarity with the *Kollektivsymbole*, a shared collection of visuals and expressions, which both writers and artists use in order to convey meaning.[45]

In the case of *Punch*, the magazine relied on an inherited canon of expressions and satirical tropes that had already been familiar visual symbols by the early eighteenth century.[46] These were the personification of nations into emblematic figures, such as John Bull or John Chinaman, or anthropomorphisation, such as the British lion or the Chinese dragon, and these figures were imbued with codes of national characteristics familiar to viewers. John Bull, for example, represented honesty, sensibility, fairness, and was fiercely loyal to King – or Queen, and country. *Punch* often employed John Bull as he was a well-established figure; he was even *Punch*-ified when the magazine's artist, John Tenniel, illustrated the allegorical figure with the face of their genial editor, Mark Lemon.[47] *Punch* artists also drew from established iconography, representing nations from animals drawn from heraldry and commenting on global encounters and politics through well-loved fairy tales or allusions to Shakespeare and Dickens.[48]

Another familiar visual metaphor frequently used is that of sleeping nations. Since the late eighteenth century in English language publications, caricaturists began to employ visual metaphor to depict a nation's perceived state of being by classifying people into a collective category attributed with historical agency.[49] Allegorical figures representing nations could be shown "asleep" to denote a lack of modernity and the absence of people's sense of resolve and determination to progress their country; or they might be represented as "sick" in order to convey the notion of a nation's inability to mobilise and strengthen itself.[50]

Punch's depiction of China and the Ottoman Empire in 1898 as "sick men" illustrates perceptions of inertia and decay (Figure 1.2). The cartoon interacted with textual descriptions as well as other visual understandings of China that was disseminated to the public, a reiteration that resulted in the embedding and normalisation of ideas. *The North-China Herald*, for example, published an article titled "The Disease of China" and used the metaphor of "chronic disease" throughout to explain China's surprising defeat in the First Sino-Japanese war of 1894–1895.[51]

FIGURE 1.2 "Another 'Sick Man'" *Punch*, Vol. 114 (8 January 1898), p. 7.

Source: Punch, or The London Charivari

While there were important developments in cartooning during the eighteenth century, it was in the nineteenth century that cartoons and caricatures combined forces with imperialism to have a global influence. Cartoons are invaluable source materials for understanding imperialism because "they themselves emerged from imperial contexts."[52] *Punch* was only one of many influential and popular newspapers and magazines and its exclusive focus can, as Richard Scully and Henry Miller quite rightly point out, be counterproductive.[53] *Punch* was, however, an important vehicle in the node of information exchange and intricately connected with the British Empire. The widespread popularity of the magazine not only enabled its home audience to engage with imperialism, but it also forged a connection between Britain and its readers in the colonies, contributing to a complex and significant web of communication. *Punch* therefore makes an interesting case study to view the prism of imperialism, knowledge production, and dissemination, as well as the persuasion and crystallisation of particular notions and attitudes.

The case study

Punch *as a historical source*

As a historical source, *Punch* is unique due to its widespread popularity and influence. Scholars often refer to the magazine as a national institution[54] in the Victorian era and its circulation numbers, global influence, and longevity[55] mark as one of the most successful magazine of the English-speaking world from its inaugural issue in 1841 until its last publication in 2002.[56] The magazine was quoted in *The Times* as well as the House of Commons and was read by notable figures such as Charlotte Brontë, Robert Browning, Henry James, C.S. Lewis, Queen Victoria, and Prince Albert.[57] There is also a testament of *Punch* readers extending beyond the middle and upper classes. For example, in Wales, when the Prime Minister Lord Palmerston was addressed by a mail carrier, the surprised politician asked how he knew him and the postman replied "Seen your picture in *Punch*, my lord."[58] Thomas Carlyle complained that when he visited Scotland, people "pestered [him] with questions as to who it was that wrote this, that, and the other thing in *Punch*."[59]

Of course, the publication of a magazine or an article does not necessarily mean that they are actually read, nor does it mean that the reader agrees with the content. In regard to actual number of readers, scholars on Victorian periodicals give a conservative estimate of the ratio of readers to copies as five to one.[60] Table 1.1 has the first issue at 20,000 copies; however, the first print run was 10,000 with two additional print runs of 5,000 due to high demand.

TABLE 1.1 *Punch* Circulation Table

Year	*Total copies*	*Total readers*
1841 (first edition)	20,000	100,000
1841 (September)	6,000	30,000
1842	c. 30,000	150,000
1844	22,795	113,975

(*Continued*)

TABLE 1.1 (Continued)

Year	*Total copies*	*Total readers*
1845	43,220	216,100
1846	48,990	244,950
1847	39,335	196,675
1848	37,535	187,675
1849	33,255	166,275
1850	33,180	165,900
1854	48,000	240,000
1885	c. 50,000	250,000
1905 (November)	61,000	305,000

The table does not record how many subscribers shared their issue with friends and family members or how many people pored over the magazine in public establishments such as coffee houses or gentlemen's clubs where an assortment of news prints, including *Punch*, was displayed for the enjoyment of their guests.[61] One example is found in George Orwell's *Burmese Days*, a novel based on Orwell's experiences as a policeman in Burma. He mentions "Dear old *Punch*" as one of the English papers brought into The European Club for the colonial officers.[62]

The circulation of the magazine extended beyond Britain. In 1883, Henry James wrote, "Many people in the United States gathered their knowledge of English life almost entirely from *Punch*," to which he added, "and it would be difficult to imagine a more abundant, and on the whole more accurate, informant."[63] In France and Germany, the magazine on-and-off bans with varying degrees of censorship.

In 1894, Tenniel's French wolf about to spring upon a Madagascar lamb as visual commentary on French colonial expansion aroused indignation from Britain's continental neighbours (Figure 1.3). In Germany, Kaiser Wilhelm II withdrew his subscriptions to the magazine, as well as those of members of the royal family when he took offence to *Punch*'s rendition of the struggle between the Emperor and the Reichstag. As a response, Sambourne illustrated the Kaiser as *Struwwelpeter*, angrily ripping up *Punch* magazines as he stands among his toys scattered and thrown around the nursery as a result of his temper tantrum (Figure 1.4).

The Russians fared no better under *Punch*'s satirical attacks and the magazine kept the Russian censors busy destroying potentially offensive cartoons of the Tsar and his country's foreign policy. When Sambourne travelled to Russia, he remarked, "Should it happen . . . that any cartoon or cut at all trenched on Russian subjects, and especially his Majesty the Tsar, the page was either torn out or erased in the blackest manner by the Bear's paw."

FIGURE 1.3 "Nobody Looking" *Punch*, Vol. 107 (24 November 1894), p. 247.

Source: Punch, or The London Charivari

Sambourne subsequently took the opportunity to illustrate his observations in a cartoon titled "Under the Censor's Stamp" (Figure 1.5). On another occasion, the ambassador to Russia, Lord Augustus Loftus, recalled an incident on the eve of the Russo-Turkish War, when he met the Tsar, seated in an inner saloon near a table with a number of *Punch* magazines. He picked up a cartoon representing Austria, Russia, and Germany at a gambling table with the Tsar holding down his hand with a card (Figure 1.6). He then turned to the Ambassador and demanded "*Expliquez-moi cela*" to which Lord Loftus "felt the difficulty of the situation" and after collecting his thoughts, replied "your Majesty is represented apparently as hesitating whether to continue the game."[64]

These anecdotes, from the mail carrier addressing Lord Palmerston to the French, German, and Russian reactions to *Punch* not only highlight the widespread distribution of the magazine both nationally and internationally, but they also give us a rare glimpse into how some audiences reacted to these images. The anecdotes also underscore *Punch* as an integral vehicle in transnational flows of information, knowledge, opinions, ideas, and cultural influence and its widespread dissemination was made possible with the thriving print media industry. The Victorians witnessed new forms of communication technologies such as technical developments in mass printing and the telegraph, systems that

FIGURE 1.4 "Wilful Wilhelm" *Punch*, Vol. 102 (26 March 1892), p. 146.

Source: Punch, or The London Charivari

re-conceptualised the sense of temporality as the degree of speed in relaying information of events happening in far-away places accelerated.

The British Empire contributed to a re-evaluation of geographical space as once "unknown, distant, foreign" lands and people were colonised and information made its way back to Britain either as texts or in forms of visual and material culture. News flowed into Britain and was then disseminated out to the home audience through one of the estimated 50,000 periodicals or newspapers during the Victorian era.[65] Simon Potter claims that, arguably, the press "was *the* single most important institution acting to define the limits for the acceptable

UNDER THE CENSOR'S STAMP;
OR, HOW THE BEAR'S PAW COMES DOWN ON PUNCH IN ST. PETERSBURG. AND YET THE JINGOES CALL HIM "RUSSOPHIL"!

FIGURE 1.5 "Under the Censor's Stamp" *Punch*, Vol. 75 (23 November 1878), p. 230.

Source: Punch, or The London Charivari

integration of the British world in the late nineteenth and early twentieth centuries."[66]

Punch was entirely dependent on the media for material to satirise and scanned the daily press, relying especially on *The Times*. The magazine itself as well as the individual men that staffed *Punch* formed an intricate discursive network of interactive communications of opinions, ideas, and notions, and of fierce criticism within and between the social and political Victorian world. As will be further discussed in the next chapter, the editors, writers, and artists were of differing political persuasions, therefore the politics of *Punch* continually re-negotiated and re-defined its position on particular topics and frequently allowed for tensions and intersections to exist between texts and images.

Punch's attractive and entertaining cartoons along with the interspersed witty text resulted in a dynamic repository of the most talked-about and of-the-moment topics of the day. The magazine was used as a benchmark for satirical journals and

FIGURE 1.6 "A Break in the Game" *Punch*, Vol. 71 (28 October 1876), p. 181.

Source: Punch, or The London Charivari

was picked up and restyled by various countries around the world, each modifying the humour to suit their own political and cultural environments.[67] The format of *Punch* thus came into contact with diverse artists and writers from around the world, who utilised and adapted imported methods and technologies to pursue and disseminate their own agendas. Meiji Japan, for example, merged their indigenous art form with the *Ponchi-e* picture (translation meaning: "*Punch* picture").[68]

It is unsurprising that scholars exploring aspects of Victorian Britain continue to find *Punch* as an invaluable source when investigating multifarious topics ranging from the perceived threat of Catholicism, slavery in America, and other policies in effect both at home and abroad.[69] The magazine's history along with its illustrious editors, writers, and artists has also been subjects of interest. Spielmann's research is arguably the most comprehensible study to date. Published in 1895, *The History of Punch* is a monumental work on the internal functioning of the magazine and offers its readers a unique and intimate glance into the inner workings as Spielmann consulted surviving members of staff from the 1850s and 1860s and had access to materials now no longer available.[70] In 1921, Charles L. Graves wrote four volumes, each titled *Mr. Punch's History of Modern England*. More recent works include Richard Altick's impressive 1997 study on the first ten years of *Punch*'s history and Patrick Leary's 2010 *The Punch Brotherhood*, which examines the diverse and often conflicting personalities of the magazine.

Despite the interest the magazine continues to hold, what is missing from this discourse is an analysis of caricatures of the Chinese. This project hopes to fill the gap in the historiography of *Punch*-ology that has to date no thorough examination of the series of satirical commentaries the magazine created of China and the Chinese throughout the Victorian era. The cartoons that do make it into scholarly studies tend to be highly selective and used only as supporting source materials to the central argument. The following chapters depart from previous scholarship that work with selected samples of *Punch* cartoons in order to buttress an argument, moving away from the propensity for selectivity that, as Richard Scully states, "plagues the use of cartoons in historical scholarship."[71] Such selecting can misconstrue and underestimate diversity of opinions as well as obscure the complexities in which China was discussed at a tumultuous time in the history of Sino-British relations.

The framework of understanding

Contextualising Punch

Mid-nineteenth-century Britain experienced cracks in the foundation of established hierarchal divisions of class and race. Beginning in the late 1830s, the Chartist movement was the first mass movement of the working classes demanding political rights and its rise came at a time of violent revolutions throughout Europe. At the same time, new notions of progress and civilisation shaped ideological perspectives over other nations while theories on race consigned non-Europeans to an inferior status.[72] The press was instrumental in the movement of ideas and provided a popular and powerful medium enabling readers to engage with new cultures. Illustrated periodicals printed a diversity of visuals: images of bodies, architectures, and landscapes of far-away places and people that reaffirmed concepts of identities. The press also disseminated a vast range of multivoiced expressions regarding an endless array of topics, including nuanced political debates legitimising or critiquing various wars and foreign policies.[73]

In regard to China, there was an exchange of ideas and opinions between the press in Britain and the British living in China who expressed their experiences in either one of the English-language newspapers that circulated within the foreign community or by sending in a contribution to a "home" newspaper. Sascha Auerbach notes that despite the tales of violence and atrocities, such as the Boxer Uprising, that found its way back to London, the event in the British press was rarely mentioned in connection to the Chinese neighbourhoods in Britain. Rather, nineteenth-century public opinion on the Chinese occupied Bhabha's ambivalent space, oscillating between admiration and derision. Some commended the Chinese to be a hard-working and peace-loving people while others expressed contempt for what they perceived as insalubrious communities and immoral behaviour. There was, therefore, no static representation of the

Chinese and Victorian writers and journalists provided a fluid, fragmented, and at times contradictory narrative.[74]

Charles Dicken's *The Mystery of Edwin Drood* (1870) and Oscar Wilde's *The Picture of Dorian Grey* (1890) depict London's Chinatown opium dens as a source of exotic fascination and horror; Walter Besant's 1899 visit to an opium den records his disappointment. He declared that the only "horror of the opium den" was "the intolerable music" that was playing in the background.[75] There was also an assortment of visual and material culture that dispersed information on and about China and the Chinese. The research of Elizabeth Hope Chang and Catherine Pagani argues that visuals, such as objects, artefacts, and commodities that took shape in a variety of forms, including as exhibitions or as porcelain, shaped British attitudes and notions about China. Both Chang and Pagani demonstrate the intricate connection between the ocular experience and racial constructions of the Chinese, where differences were emphasised and stood as a negative contrast to Britain's sense of itself as a superior nation.[76]

Sarah Cheang's research on London department shops offers yet another example of China's fluctuating perception in Britain. While China was being carved up by various rival imperial powers in the closing decade of the nineteenth century, luxury Chinese items were being sold to British consumers. Cheang argues that London's West End shops became imperial spaces where Chinese products were sold as an expression of colonial nostalgia for "old China" and contributed to British class identities.[77] These visual and textual forms of information about China must have made an impact to the majority of Britons who would have never had the opportunity to travel to China or interact with a Chinese person. During his disappointing visit to London's Limehouse, Besant estimated that there could not have been "more than a hundred Chinese, or thereabouts" noting that compared to the Chinese community in New York, "that of London is a small thing and of no importance."[78] Besant was correct in his appraisal; by the 1890s, the China-born population in London numbered only around three hundred.[79]

Within this environment where the Chinese were at once invisible and little understood, the cartoons that *Punch* created using repetitive frameworks of visual tropes perpetuated and reinforced established stereotypes of the Chinese within the popular British imagination. Visual representations of the Chinese from 1841 to 1901 remained relatively static with *Punch* employing age-old lexicon of stereotypes; however, the textual accompaniment and message in the cartoon shifted according to developments in British politics in relation to China. China appeared as early as 1842 in a *Punch* Large Cut titled, "The Presentation of the Chinese Ambassador." These Large Cuts, discussed in more detail in Chapter 3, were the most important cartoon in each weekly volume. What merited such a cut was chosen by the "hottest" topic that made headlines in the daily press and was not only too pressing for *Punch* to ignore, but events would also have been at the very forefront of public consciousness, which is essential for creating comprehensible satirical cartoons.

TABLE 1.2 Large Cut Cartoons of China and the Chinese

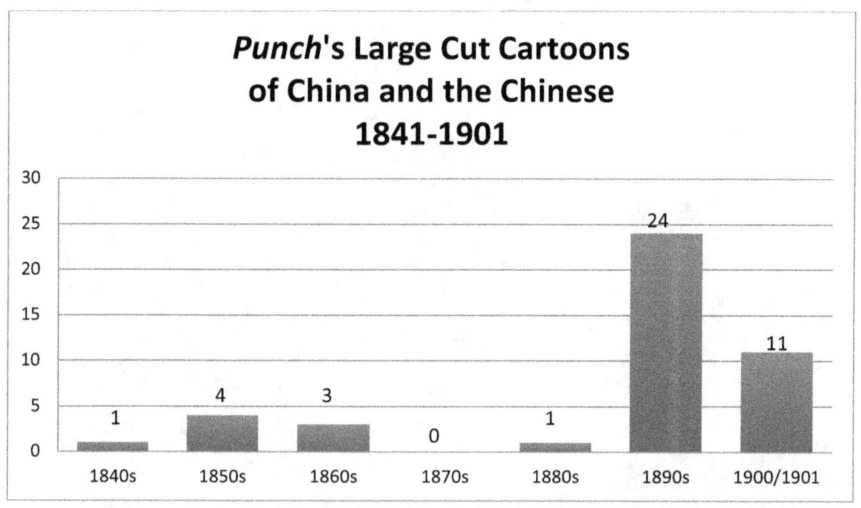

* 1901: ends with the death of Queen Victoria on 22 January 1901.

If the Large Cuts could be used as an indicator of the topics that preoccupied a certain segment of Victorian society, then interest in China remained minimal except for spikes during the 1850s and 1860s that coincided with the Second Opium War. By the 1890s, there was a dramatic increase which corresponded to the First Sino-Japanese war of 1894–1895. As explored in Chapter 5, the conflict between China and Japan captured British interest. The Large Cuts in the final years of the nineteenth century focused on imperial rivalries and Britain's global standing, more so than any relationship, socio-cultural or political, with China. Table 1.2 displays *Punch*'s Large Cuts of China from 1841 to 1901.

The following chapters are organised chronologically to trace the downward trajectory of *Punch*'s narrative of China and the Chinese people that was directly linked to fluctuations in Britain's relationship with China. The 1870s and 1880s are not examined due to the magazine's almost non-existing number of Large Cuts of China found in those two decades. This does not mean, however, that Britain was not engaged with China nor that China did not feature in the daily news. The Sino-French war (1883–1885), for example, was satirised in blurbs and even made "the cut," as in the Large Cut, in September 1883 where Madam France is depicted receiving advice from John Bull that developing a taste for China was a very expensive pursuit (Figure 1.7).

Other references to China during the 1870s and 1880s include satirical attacks on British and Chinese merchants who traded and sold adulterated tea to British consumers. While important, these issues in the following chapters are not discussed if *Punch* did not offer sufficient visual and textual material for examination.

"CHINAMANIA."

FIGURE 1.7 "Chinamania" *Punch*, Vol. 85 (15 September 1883), p. 127.

Source: Punch, or The London Charivari

Chapter 2 explores the idiosyncrasies of the editors and individual staff members behind the magazine. The aim is to examine the intellectual and political underpinnings of *Punch* to offer readers an in-depth understanding of the men who came together to create this magazine. Chapter 3 investigates the magazine as a finished product. It discusses the layout, content, and tone with special attention given to the Large Cut cartoon. Chapter 4 highlights the evolution of negative perceptions towards China. Within British society, there was a whirlwind of socio-political shifts and changes, circulation of new ideas and concepts, and introduction to foreign cultures and peoples. In soothing any potential fears, *Punch* provided guiding principles of behaviour and appropriateness between different sectors of British society. During the Great Exhibition of 1851, disruptions in social and racial hierarchies gave rise to anxieties and *Punch* poked fun at social mixing between the separate classes. At the same time, the magazine instilled a sense of identity and belonging when confronted with foreignness and notions of "Chineseness" were an ideal foil to ideas of "Britishness." By the end of the Second Opium War, *Punch* was clear in its anti-Chinese standpoint and created emotive cartoons to clearly convey its sentiments to its readers. Chapter 5 examines heightened tensions and anxieties with the sudden shift in geopolitics after the First Sino-Japanese war. This affected not only Britain's standing in China but also its position as an imperial power on the international arena.

Throughout the chapters, I use the terms "Britain" rather than "England" as well as "China" rather than "Manchu" or "Han" when I am referring to a cartoon with allegorical figures because they were created using "a conglomeration of value judgements" to represent nations, which "the Victorians were so fond of applying to whole regions and countries."[80] This is, of course, an oversimplification; the lion, for example, used to represent Britain makes no distinction, say, between England and Scotland or England and Wales. The same applies to China represented as a dragon, which makes no attempt to recognise the Manchu ruling elite's ethnic difference with the majority Han population or the multitude of ethnic minorities that lived in China. Regardless, *Punch* provides an interesting case study in deciphering the socio-cultural tempo of daily life as well as Britain's perpetually evolving global conjunctures. *Punch* occupied a central role in the evolution of public thought and its caricatures of the Chinese form a useful counterpoint to explore the complexities, contradictions, and multifaceted symbols of China in the popular British imagination.

Notes

1 M. H. Spielmann, *The History of "Punch"* (London: Cassell & Company, Limited), p. 111.
2 Dominic Williams, "*Punch* and the Pogroms: Eastern Atrocities in John Tenniel's Political Cartoons, 1876–1896" *RACAR: Revue d'art Canadienne / Canadian Art Review*, Vol. 42, No. 1 (2017), p. 32.
3 Richard Scully and Andrekos Varnava, "Introduction: The Importance of Cartoons, Caricature, and Satirical Art in Imperial Contexts" *Comic Empires: Imperialism in Cartoons, Caricature and Satirical Art* (eds.) Richard Scully and Andrekos Varnava (Manchester: Manchester University Press, 2019), p. 5.
4 J. P. May, "The Chinese in Britain, 1860–1914" *Immigrants and Minorities in British Society* (ed.) Colin Holmes (London: Allen and Unwin, 1978), p. 111; Jeffrey A. Auerback, *The Great Exhibition of 1851: A Nation on Display* (New Haven, CT: Yale University Press, 1999), p. 186.
5 Sascha Auerbach, *Race, Law, and "The Chinese Puzzle" in Imperial Britain* (New York: Palgrave Macmillan, 2009), p. 6.

6 Scully and Varnava, "Introduction" p. 6.
7 Kylie Message and Ewan Johnston, "The World Within the City: The Great Exhibition, Race, Class and Social Reform" *Britain, the Empire, and the World at the Great Exhibition of 1851* (eds.) Jeffrey A. Auerback and Peter H. Hoffenberg (Burlington, VT: Ashgate, 2008), p. 29.
8 Edward Said, *Orientalism* (New York: Vintage Books, 1979), p. 3.
9 Said, *Orientalism*, pp. 26, 86.
10 Homi K. Bhabha, "The Other Question: Stereotype, Discrimination and the Discourse of Colonialism" *The Location of Culture* (London: Routledge, 1994), p. 66.
11 Bhabha, "The Other Question" pp. 67–70.
12 Virginia Richter, "Laughter and Aggression: Desire and Derision in a Postcolonial Context" *Cheeky Fictions* (eds.) Susanne Reichl and Mark Stein (Amsterdam; New York: Rodopi, 2005), p. 64.
13 Arif Dirlik, "Chinese History and the Question of Orientalism," *History and Theory*, Vol. 35, No. 4, Theme Issue 35: Chinese Historiography in Comparative Perspective (December 1996), p. 99.
14 Cited in Scully and Varnava, "Introduction" p. 6.
15 Said, *Orientalism*, p. 325.
16 Simon J. Potter, "Communication and Integration: The British and Dominions Press and the British World, c.1876–1914" *The Journal of Imperial and Commonwealth History*, Vol. 31, No. 2 (2003), pp. 193–194.
17 Jürgen Habermas, *The Structural Transformation of the Public Sphere*, translated by Thomas Burger with the assistance of Frederick Lawrence (Cambridge: Polity Press, 1989), pp. 193–194.
18 George Somes Layard, *The Life and Letters of Charles Samuel Keene of "Punch"* (London: Sampson Low, Marston & Company, Limited, 1893), p. 51.
19 John Berger, *Ways of Seeing* (London: British Broadcasting Corporation in association with Penguin Books, 1972), p. 33.
20 Victor S. Navasky, *The Art of Controversy: Political Cartoons and Their Enduring Power* (New York: Alfred A. Knopf, 2013), pp. 35–36.
21 Layard, *The Life and Letters of Charles Samuel Keene of "Punch,"* p. 50.
22 Christopher Kent, "War Cartooned / Cartoon War: Matt Morgan and the American Civil War in 'Fun' and 'Frank Leslie's Illustrated Newspaper'" *Victorian Periodicals Review*, Vol. 36, No. 2 (Summer 2003), p. 154.
23 Henry James, *The Painter's Eye*, edited by John L. Sweeney (London: Rupert Hart-Davis, 1956), p. 229.
24 Habermas, *The Structural Transformation of the Public Sphere*, p. 194.
25 It was *Punch* artist John Leech who first coined the term "cartoon" in the 1840s in reference to his satirical drawings for the magazine and the word later came to incorporate all humorous drawings. Patrick Leary, *The Punch Brotherhood: Table Talk and Print Culture in Mid-Victorian London* (London: The British Library, 2010), p. 35; "An Introduction" *PUNCH Magazine Cartoon Archive*. Online: http://www.punch.co.uk/about/.
26 Diana Donald, *The Age of Caricature: Satirical Prints in the Reign of George III* (New Haven; London: Yale University Press, 1996), pp. 15–19.
27 Peter Burke, *Eyewitnessing: The Uses of Images as Historical Evidence* (London: Reaktion Books Limited, 2001), p. 141.
28 Donald, *The Age of Caricature*, p. 14.
29 Spielmann, *The History of "Punch,"* p. 205.
30 "ce qui rappelle instantanément, pleinement, c'est beaucoup moins ce qui est semblable a l'objet lui-même, que ce qui est semblable a l'idée que nous avons de l'objet." Translation and emphasis mine. Rodolphe Töpffer, *De la plaque Daguerre: À propos des Excursions daguerriennes* (Cognac: Le temps qu'il fait, 2002), p. 61.
31 "quatre jambs fines, une panse ample, une queue maigre et deux longues oreilles." Translation mine. Töpffer, *De la plaque Daguerre*, pp. 61–62.

32 Navasky, *The Art of Controversy*, pp. 44–46.
33 Scully and Varnava, "Introduction" p. 6.
34 Cited in Spielmann, *The History of "Punch,"* p. 189.
35 Scully and Varnava, "Introduction" p. 7.
36 William Murrell, *A History of American Graphic Humor*, Vol. 2 (New York, 1938), p. 46, cited in Martha Banta, *Barbaric Intercourse: Caricature and the Culture of Conduct, 1841–1936* (Chicago; London: The University of Chicago Press, 2003), p. 4; also cited in Navasky, *The Art of Controversy*, p. 43.
37 E. B. White, "Some Remarks on Humor" adapted from *A Subtreasury of American Humor*, 1941, p. 244 cited in *In the Words of E.B. White: Quotations from America's Most Companionable of Writers*, edited by Martha White (Ithaca: Cornell University Press, 2011), p. 129.
38 Spielmann, *The History of "Punch,"* p. 463.
39 Mark Twain, *The Mysterious Stranger and Other Stories* (New York; London: Harper & Brothers Publishers, 1922), p. 132.
40 Ronald Dworkin, "The Right to Ridicule" *The New York Review of Books* (23 March 2006). Online: https://www.nybooks.com/articles/2006/03/23/the-right-to-ridicule.
41 Scully and Varnava, "Introduction" pp. 9–10.
42 Walter Benjamin, *Illuminations*, translation by Harry Zohn (New York: Schocken, 1969), p. 89, cited in David Spurr, *The Rhetoric of Empire: Colonial Discourse in Journalism, Travel Writing, and Imperial Administration* (Durham; London: Duke University Press, 1993), pp. 8–9.
43 Navasky, *The Art of Controversy*, p. 39.
44 Burke, *Eyewitnessing*, p. 14.
45 Rudolf G. Wagner, "China 'Asleep' and 'Awakening': A Study in Conceptualizing Asymmetry and Coping with It" *Transcultural Studies*, No. 1 (2011), p. 9.
46 Donald, *The Age of Caricature*, p. 47.
47 Spielmann, *The History of "Punch,"* p. 206; Richard D. Altick, *Punch: The Lively Youth of a British Institution, 1841–1851* (Columbus: Ohio State University, 1997), pp. 138–139.
48 Robert Dingley and Richard Scully, "Courting the Colonies: Linley Sambourne, *Punch*, and Imperial Allegory" *Comic Empires: Imperialism in Cartoons, Caricature and Satirical Art* (eds.) Richard Scully and Andrekos Varnava (Manchester: Manchester University Press, 2019), p. 31.
49 Wagner, "China 'Asleep' and 'Awakening,'" p. 55.
50 Wagner, "China 'Asleep' and 'Awakening,'" pp. 37–38, 56–57.
51 "The Disease of China" *The North-China Herald* (Shanghai) (10 August 1894), p. 219.
52 Scully and Varnava, "Introduction" p. 13.
53 Richard Scully, *British Images of Germany: Admiration, Antagonism & Ambivalence, 1860–1914* (Basingstoke: Palgrave Macmillan, 2012), p. 136; Henry Miller, "The Problem with Punch" *Institute of Historical Research*, Vol. 82, No. 216 (May 2009), pp. 285–302.
54 To name just a few: Frank E. Huggett, *Victorian England as Seen by Punch* (London: Book Club Associates, 1978), p. 7; Leary, *The Punch Brotherhood*, p. 1; Banta, *Barbaric Intercourse*, p. 2; Stanley Appelbaum and Richard Kelly (eds.), *Great Drawings and Illustrations from Punch, 1841–1901* (New York: Dover Publications, Inc., 1981), p. IX.
55 Apart for some interruptions, *Punch* was published for over 160 years.
56 Leary, *The Punch Brotherhood*, pp. 1–2; Hans Harder, "Prologue: Late Nineteenth and Twentieth Century Asian Punch Versions and Related Satirical Journals" *Asian Punches, A Transcultural Affair* (eds.) Hans Harder and Barbara Mittler (Heidelberg: Springer, 2013), p. 1; "History of Punch" on *PUNCH Magazine Cartoon Archive*. Online: http://www.punch.co.uk/about/.
57 Altick, *Punch*, pp. XVII–XX.
58 Spielmann, *The History of "Punch,"* p. 203.
59 Spielmann, *The History of "Punch,"* p. 19.

60 The figures for the years 1841, 1842, 1885 and 1905 are taken from Punch Magazine Cartoon Archive, "About" on www.punch.co.uk/about/index. I have calculated the total readers based on the five to one ratio. The figures for the years 1844 to 1854 are cited in Altick, *Punch*, p. 38.
61 Altick, *Punch*, p. 39.
62 George Orwell, *Burmese Days* (London: Penguin in association with Martin Secker and Warburg, 1989), p. 17. I am grateful to Paul Bevan for bringing this reference to my attention.
63 Henry James, *Partial Portraits* (London; New York: Macmillan and Co., 1894), p. 333.
64 Spielmann, *The History of "Punch,"* pp. 191–195.
65 Alexis Easley, Andrew King and John Morton, "Introduction" *Researching the Nineteenth-Century Periodical Press: Case Studies* (eds.) Alexis Easley, Andrew King and John Morton (London: Routledge, Taylor & Francis Group, 2018), E-books online at the British Library, n.p.
66 Potter, "Communication and Integration" p. 191.
67 See Hans Harder, *Asian Punches, A Transcultural Affair* (eds.) Hans Harder and Barbara Mittler (Heidelberg: Springer, 2013).
68 Scully and Varnava, "Introduction" p. 13.
69 To name just a few studies: on the Irish: Joseph P. Finnan, "Punch's Portrayal of Redmond, Carson and the Irish Question, 1910–18" *Irish Historical Studies*, Vol. 33, No. 132 (November 2003), pp. 424–445; Peter Gray, "Punch and the Great Famine" *History Ireland*, Vol. 1, No. 2 (Summer 1993), pp. 26–33; On Slavery in America: Michael A. Chaney, "Heartfelt Thanks to Punch for the Picture: Frederick Douglass and the Transnational Jokework of Slave Caricature" *American Literature*, Vol. 82, No. 1 (March 2010), pp. 57–90; Oscar Maurer, "'Punch' on Slavery and Civil War in America" *Victorian Studies*, Vol. 1, No. 1 (September 1957), pp. 4–28; On Eastern Europeans: Katarzyna Murawska-Muthesius, "On Small Nations and Bullied Children: Mr. Punch Draws Eastern Europe" *The Slavonic and East European Review*, Vol. 84, No. 2 (April 2006), pp. 279–305; On the Pope: Eleanor McNees, "'Punch' and the Pope: Three Decades of Anti-Catholic Caricature" *Victorian Periodicals Review*, Vol. 37, No. 1 (Spring 2004), pp. 18–45; On King Arthur: Roger Simpson, "King Arthur at the 'Punch' Round Table, 1859–1914" *Arthuriana*, Vol. 9, No. 4 (Winter 1999), pp. 94–115.
70 Leary, *The Punch Brotherhood*, p. 2.
71 Richard Scully, "A Pettish Little Emperor" *Drawing the Line: Using Cartoons as Historical Evidence* (eds.) Richard Scully and Marian Quartly (Clayton, Victoria: Monash University ePress, 2009). Online: http://books.publishing.monash.edu. (Accessed 11 May 2018); also in Richard Scully and Marian Quartly, "Using Cartoons as Historical Evidence" *Drawing the Line: Using Cartoons as Historical Evidence* (eds.) Richard Scully and Marian Quartly (Clayton, Victoria: Monash University ePress, 2009). Online: http://books.publishing.monash.edu. (Accessed 11 May 2018).
72 Gregory Blue, "China and Western Social Thought in the Modern Period" *China and Historical Capitalism: Genealogies of Sinological Knowledge* (eds.) Timothy Brook and Gregory Blue (Cambridge: Cambridge University Press, 1999), pp. 75–78.
73 Julie F. Codell, "Introduction" *Imperial Co-Histories: National Identities and the British and Colonial Press* (ed.) Julie F. Codell (Madison, NJ: Fairleigh Dickinson University Press; London: Associated University Presses, 2003), p. 18.
74 Auerbach, *Race, Law, and "The Chinese Puzzle" in Imperial Britain*, pp. 4–8.
75 Walter Besant, *East London* (London: Chatto & Windus, 1901), pp. 205–206.
76 Elizabeth Hope Chang, *Britain's Chinese Eye* (Stanford, CA: Stanford University Press, 2010); Catherine Pagani, "Chinese Material Culture and British Perceptions of China in the Mid-Nineteenth Century" *Colonialism and the Object: Empire, Material Culture and the Museum* (eds.) Tim Barringer and Tom Flynn (London: Routledge, 1998), pp. 28–40; Catherine Pagani, "Objects and the Press: Images of China in Nineteenth-Century

Britain" *Imperial Co-Histories* (ed.) Julie F. Codell (Madison, NJ; London: Fairleigh Dickinson University Press, 2003), pp. 147–166.
77 Sarah Cheang, "Selling China: Class, Gender and Orientalism at the Department Store" *Journal of Design History*, Vol. 20, No. 1 (Spring 2007), pp. 1–16.
78 Besant, *East London*, p. 204.
79 Auerbach, *Race, Law, and "The Chinese Puzzle" in Imperial Britain*, p. 6.
80 L. Perry Curtis, Jr. *Apes and Angels: The Irishman in Victorian Caricature* (Newton Abbot: David & Charles, Ltd., 1971), p. 2.

2

"GENTLEMEN, THE CARTOON!"

The men behind the magazine

In July 1891, *Punch* artist Edward Linley Sambourne created an image of the men behind the magazine toasting a statue of Mr. Punch at a Jubilee dinner. The staff had reason to celebrate: in less than four years, the magazine became "the most talked-about and enjoyed periodical of its time"[1] and by the 1890s, many considered *Punch* an important Victorian institution. It all began on 17 July 1841, when three writers, Mark Lemon, Henry Mayhew, and Stirling Coyne, along with engraver Ebenezer Landells, and a printer, Joseph Last, decided to launch a new satirical magazine called *Punch; or The London Charivari*. There are many stories concerning how the magazine got its name; however, a popular re-telling is when "someone" spoke of the paper as "a good mixture of punch, being nothing without Lemon" to which Mayhew cried out "A capital idea! We'll call it *Punch*!"[2] Thereafter, "Mister Punch," with his hunched back and hooked nose, was decided upon as the representative and voice of the magazine. He was the cartoon version of the popular and much-loved glove puppet that first appeared in London as street entertainment at the turn of the nineteenth century.

Mr. Punch's original murderous and wife-beating temper amused both children and adults but by mid-century, his temper was tamed and the stories of Mr. Punch and his wife Judy had a moral message for children as domesticity and gender roles became increasingly linked with notions of respectability.[3] The decision to incorporate him as the magazine's mascot was ingenious. Mr. Punch was a familiar and much-loved folk icon and evoked fond memories of childhood, seaside resorts, and happy holidays for many of the magazine's readers.[4] Lemon would later explain the reason for the name of the magazine, "It was called *Punch* because it was short and sweet. And Punch is an English institution. Everyone loves Punch, and will be drawn aside to listen to it. All our ideas connected with Punch are happy ones."[5]

DOI: 10.4324/9781003025573-2

FIGURE 2.1 "The Mahogany Tree" *Punch*, Vol. 101 (18 July 1891), pp. 31–32.

Source: Punch, or The London Charivari

With the launch of the magazine, a weekly Wednesday evening dinner was established in order for members to enjoy a meal together and discuss the contents of the week's Large Cut cartoon while passing around brandy and cigars. The call to attention was the editor's announcement: "Gentlemen, the cartoon!" (Figure 2.1), titled "The Mahogany Tree," was in reference to the song that one member, Horace Mayhew, was fond of singing at special *Punch* dinners.[6] The image captures a sense of camaraderie between the men, represented by the pineapple prominently displayed at the centre of the table, the traditional symbol of friendship and hospitality. What is glossed over in this picture-perfect representation is the suppressed animosity between some members of staff as well as the initial bumps at the start of the magazine's career.

Despite the magazine's early success, *Punch* soon found itself in a precarious position due to mounting financial troubles and Last parted ways with the magazine. To stave off mounting debts, Lemon and Mayhew approached William Bradbury and Frederick Evans in December 1842 to persuade the businessmen to purchase the magazine for little more than its debts. Bradbury and Evans had built a successful printing firm based on the latest technology as well as expertise in woodcut illustrations. With their support and business savvy, *Punch* editors and members of staff were able to fully concentrate their energies on the creation of witty content and attractive images.[7] This change in ownership, however, was not without its challenges.

The company re-organised the magazine from a collective system into a more traditional hierarchal one and turned the small *Punch* staff into weekly, salaried employees.[8] Coyne was one of the first to go as he was considered of little use as co-editor or contributor and was found to have plagiarised a contribution from a Dublin paper.[9] Landells, a key player in the start-up of the magazine, was bought out after much painful negotiations that dragged from April to December 1842 and left the engraver feeling indignant; he not only opposed the sale but also was humiliated when he found out that he should not continue as engraver as he originally expected.[10] Then in April 1846, Mayhew left the group in bitter resentment. He, like Landells, was a founding member and was affronted when he was deposed of his role as a co-editor.[11] He accused Lemon of allowing himself "to be bought over" and although his brother Horace "Ponny" Mayhew stayed on as a contributor, Henry never quite forgave Lemon.[12]

With Bradbury and Evans as proprietors, Lemon was the sole editor and left in charge of the daily operations of the magazine. Despite the initial departures, few members of staff left the magazine in its first ten years[13] and this very small circle of men, described as "men in years but boys at heart,"[14] formed a tight-knit community that remained predominantly unchanged. It is important to note that even though the salaried staff of *Punch* consisted solely of white men, as they were the only sex and race thought capable of active agency in "reading" and "representing" the world,[15] the magazine did have female contributors.[16] Their entries were published anonymously in accordance with *Punch*'s policy for all writers, regardless of gender, and this continues to pose a challenge for scholars researching contributions from specific individuals.[17] While significant, the focus of this chapter is on the salaried staff members. It investigates the attitudes, political leanings, and friendships between the individual editors and staff members as well as the ways in which their professional lives crossed with their social networks. The aim is to explore the intellectual and political underpinnings of *Punch* and offer an in-depth understanding of the magazine's creative and decision-making authority.

The editors

The men at the helm

In 1862, Henry Silver, one of the writers at *Punch*, remarked in his diary "Now all works smoothly – the machinery is kept oiled by good feeling and good humour – and long may the Foreman have health to see that all goes right."[18] Silver's "Foreman" was Mark Lemon who was the sole editor until his death in 1870, followed by Shirley Brooks (1870–1874), Tom Taylor (1874–1880), and Sir Frances Burnand (1880–1906). Each stamped his personality and political leanings onto the general tone of the magazine, which made a significant difference in the direction and political complexion of *Punch*.

Lemon was essential in establishing the magazine's success due to his vigilance in ensuring that the content stayed away from scurrility and coincided with Victorian notions and ideas of gentility. He was said to be particularly sensitive in "his respect for religious prejudice and sentiment, except when discussing Roman Catholicism and Jesuitry."[19] This attentiveness is highlighted by a joke that was played by *Punch* staff members. The story tells of when Lemon went on holiday, he received a copy of the magazine by post and was horrified to discover "not the cartoon they had agreed upon, but another, execrable in taste and vile in execution while undoubted libels and other offences were sprinkled with hideous liberality about the pages."[20] Spielmann's point in recording this tale is to underscore the sense of fun and friendship between Lemon and *Punch* writers and artists; however, it also highlights Lemon's watchful eye over the appropriateness of the magazine's humour and his understanding of public decorum, which were key in ensuring *Punch*'s continued success.

While Lemon became known for his wit, sense of humour, and affable personality, he was also appreciated for his diplomacy in handling even the most dominating personalities and for his intuition on "public feeling."[21] His understanding of what should or should not appear in the magazine was invaluable; if in doubt, Lemon exercised caution in taking a stance, preferring to wait, and see in which direction public opinion would sway.[22] His shrewd judgement kept him and *Punch* from libel suits and likely accounted for his high salary that Bradbury and Evans willingly paid. With the founding of *Punch*, Lemon received thirty shillings a week but this increased substantially to fifteen hundred pounds a year by the time of his death. The loss of Lemon dramatically shifted the tone of the magazine, which in its first years, adapted a stance that oscillated between radicalism and respectability while seeking its readership from the conservative middle class.[23] With Shirley Brooks succeeding Lemon as an editor in 1870, *Punch* took on a more establishmentarian outlook as Brooks was an outspoken Tory.[24]

Brooks is said to have been "perhaps the most brilliant and useful all-round man who ever wrote for *Punch*."[25] He began as a journalist and reported on Parliament for the *Morning Chronicle* and wrote for the comic journal *The Man in the Moon*[26] where he frequently targeted *Punch*. His wit and sense of humour were so admired by Lemon and Douglas Jerrold, they asked him to join the staff and in 1852, Brooks agreed. He subsequently became good friends with both Jerrold and Lemon, as well as Francis Burnand and George Du Maurier, two increasingly important members of staff from the 1860s.[27]

Brooks was a "man of letters" with a sharp tongue and a sharper mind and working alongside Lemon, who was a "man of the world," the two complemented each other.[28] This did not mean, however, that Brooks shied away from society; indeed, he was a member of the Garrick Club's governing committee, a much sought-after position that symbolised one's status in English literary and intellectual life.[29] Among his colleagues at *Punch*, he was the only member familiar with the dynamic and competitive atmosphere of Parliamentary politics and wrote the popular weekly column "Essence of Parliament." He also became the cartoon suggestor-in-chief, working closely with the artist John Tenniel on the weekly Large Cuts.[30] Brooks was successful in having nine out of every ten of his suggestions accepted, an important feat as the Large Cuts were the most important and influential political cartoon that featured in the magazine.[31]

While his editorship was considered a success, Brooks' aggressive and dominating personality put an end to the democratic process.[32] He was a forceful and assertive Tory and Lemon expressed concern that Brooks' political leanings might damage *Punch*; Brooks frequently edited his own work, as well as others, to coincide with his beliefs. Patrick Leary describes Brooks as follows:

> He distrusted most members of the working class on principle, applauded the imperialistic gusto of Palmerston (a "true Englishman"), disapproved of Catholics (especially Irish ones), was outraged by the disestablishment of the Irish Church in 1869 (although utterly without religious feeling himself), felt a reflexive suspicion of Jews, [and] thought the dark races irremediably inferior.[33]

Despite Brooks' efforts to influence a change in the magazine's tone and character from radicalism to conservatism, he was met with opposition. Ponny Mayhew resentfully accused "Punch of turning Tory"[34] and complained that the magazine "is standing still – used to take the lead, but now fears to do so." Evans responded that "the times are altered, my dear Ponny, and *Punch* alters with the times."[35] Although Mayhew protested how "he [was] in a minority" in attempting to equilibrate the discourse, his dissenting voice was important. He was a long-term and respected member of the *Punch* group and his outlook no doubt would have had an impact.[36]

Punch was also a business. While the political leanings of the editors were significant in influencing the magazine, financial reasons dictated that the tone and content would coincide, or at least not severely offend, the interests and opinions of their majority readers, which was the conservative middle class. As has been observed, "Moulding opinion seemed a straightforward business – except when one was actually sitting in an editorial chair."[37] Brooks' editorship came to an end with his death in 1874 and the position was taken by the polymath Tom Taylor, a *Punch* member of staff for thirty-six years, six of which were spent as editor. Spielmann characterised Taylor's influence on the magazine as "decidedly Radical" as well as "anti-Imperial"[38] but it was during his editorship that the magazine declined in popularity.

Taylor was well liked as a person and appreciated for always encouraging and helping others; however, his humour was considered too academic in nature.[39] Outside his *Punch* duties, Taylor's impressive career included posts as Professor of English Literature (1845) and Secretary to the Board of Health (1854–1871); he was also a barrister, an active member of the Wandsworth Liberal Club, the author of over seventy plays, a passionate art critic but although a Liberal in politics, he regarded the suffrage movement with suspicion.[40] When he died in 1880, the *Punch* editorial torch was passed to Francis Burnand.

Burnand was already a known humourist when he was invited to the *Punch* Table in 1863, among some consternation over his style of "nonsense" humour.[41] Burnand became "the most prolific punster of the age" but even he had his patience tried when one eager contributor exhausted his patience and Burnand eventually wrote to the hopeful person, "For goodness' sake, send no more puns!"[42] Nevertheless, his editorship successfully re-established *Punch*'s reputation as a fun and jovial magazine. Burnand claimed to have "no political sympathies or antipathies whatever"[43] and this apparent political neutrality changed *Punch*'s tone as the magazine reflected "tolerance, political and religious, and wider sympathy than had lately been the case."[44]

Perhaps it was Burnand's conversion to Catholicism in 1858, much to his father's horror,[45] that enabled him to be tolerant of differing religious convictions and this, in turn, influenced the tone of the magazine. A.A. Milne considered *Punch* under Burnand "less intolerant of opinions with which it disagreed."[46] Burnand's editorship is often compared to the early years when *Punch* took an anti-Catholic stance during the "Papal Aggression" campaign of 1850, a position that led to the resignation of artist Richard Doyle.[47] How accurate were claims of Burnand's political neutrality? While he may have instilled more religious tolerance, the magazine he presided over had notable nationalist sentiments. Spielmann reports that Burnand was "born in 1837 – having been too gallant, it was said, to come into the world before his Queen had ascended the throne, and too loyal and zealous to delay his appearance after she had taken her place."[48] Burnand's loyalty is recorded in his own diary when he registered his affront at the satirical magazine *The Tomahawk*'s illustration of an empty chair depicting a vacant throne, a comment on an absent Queen Victoria as she mourned over the death of Prince Albert.

Burnand denounced the cartoon as "an unprovoked attack, and conceived in the worst possible taste," stating that Victoria "had not yet felt herself equal to appearing once again among her people and brightening London with her gracious presence."[49] His loyalty to Queen must have extended to country as the following chapters will reveal that there were more politically charged Large Cut cartoons of China during Burnand's editorship than at any earlier period in *Punch*.

The role of the editor was significant, especially when making final decisions on the important and influential Large Cuts. Despite Brooks domineering personality, whether his suggestion was accepted "rested with Mark Lemon and the rest of *Mr. Punch's* Cabinet Council"[50] but by the time he became editor, he ensured his own political leanings set the tone of the magazine. Yet throughout the Victorian period, *Punch* experienced shifts and changes not only in editors but also in writers and artists. The members consisted of a varied mix of wit and strong personalities resulting in a group defined by friendships and merry-making as well as friction and disagreements. The following section will examine some of the writers of the magazine and explore this mix of personalities, their relationships with each other along with the personal animosities and political clashes of opinion that occurred behind the scenes.

The authors

The witty writers

In 1866, when Lemon declared, "we have never had a serious dispute," he deliberately ignored a number of conflicts in the early years of the magazine, some serious enough to have resulted in sudden departures.[51] Spielmann also downplayed contentions among staff when he declaredthe occasional differences of opinion, and the harder knocks of wit, and sometimes, even, the still sharper encounters of temper, were all glossed over. As Thackeray remarked, "What is the use of quarrelling with a man if you have to meet him every Wednesday at dinner?"[52]
Yet despite these assertions, there were disputes among the members. Henry Silver's diary records the early years when "endless squabbles arose" due to "every writer finding fault with every article inserted in preference to his own."[53] Even the title of the magazine was objected to when Landells announced "Well, boys, the title for the new work is to be *Punch*," the declaration was met with complaints that it "was a very stupid one."[54]

With the constant bickering among staff members, Lemon played an important role in maintaining peace. Although consistently affable, he kept a sharp and watchful eye on conversations and was quick to dispel potential flare-ups.[55] A good example arose when someone brought up the name Edmund Yates with William Thackeray in the room after the heated Garrick Club Affair, in which Yates publicly attacked Thackeray's writing. Burnand records in his diary how Lemon immediately tried to turn the conversation and "attempted to throw oil on the troubled waters, which would have been effective had they been only waters. But, as it was, he threw the oil on smouldering fire, and – phew! – what a blaze!!"[56] Thackeray lost his temper and left early that evening.

Other outbursts had more severe repercussions for the magazine. One such incident involved the young artist Richard or "Dicky" Doyle who was not yet out of his teenage years when he began working for *Punch*. Doyle was a devout Irish Catholic and in 1850, he quit abruptly when the magazine launched an attack on the Pope and the doctrines of his faith. Thackeray had taken Doyle under his protective wing and was disappointed at his sudden departure.[57] In March 1851, "John Bull Beaten" expressed his dismay at Doyle's resignation while simultaneously blaming Douglas Jerrold, who felt strongly against any suggestions of a reinstatement of the Roman Catholic hierarchy in England, for *Punch*'s persistent attack and intolerance of Roman Catholics.[58]

There were also hints of anti-Irish sentiments directed at Coyne. Lemon referred contemptuously to him as "Paddy" and Jerrold commented rather harshly on his appearance, "Stirling Coyne? *I call him Filthy Lucre*!" Leech, Thackeray, and Gilbert à Beckett were anti-Semitics and Leech had a "hearty prejudice" against "Irishmen and Frenchmen."[59] Differing beliefs and "hearty prejudices" were a constant source of tension during the magazine's early years. *Punch* was staffed with strong personalities, men-about-town with many holding memberships in literary groups, gentlemen's clubs, political parties, and a variety of other social engagements.[60]

Of all the regular members, most belonged to the lower levels of the middle class with the exception of Thackeray who came from a wealthy Anglo-Indian family.[61] Each brought with them their own set of notions and opinions as well as their own vision on the direction the magazine should take and while there were certainly disagreements, there were also friendships that formed.

Ponny found a friend and ally in Jerrold as they were both radical in political opinions and the two were instrumental in shaping *Punch*'s early years when the magazine was radical in outlook. It was during this time that the magazine was said to have exhibited "more democratic outspokenness, more middle-class downrightness, and less of the Constitutional Club and drawing-room element" as the later years.[62] Certainly by the time Brooks became editor, there were no writers left that had the energy or intellectual capacity to challenge him and thus, under his influence, the politics of *Punch* shifted.[63] Burnand, who joined *Punch* in 1863, remembers Ponny as "comparatively silent" during political debates except when goaded by Brooks to give his opinion as a "professing Red Republican."[64] However, in the beginning before Brooks, it was Jerrold who dominated with his "admixture of Radicalism and his Whiggery."[65]

Jerrold took the opportunity to use *Punch* as a platform to express his opinions on subjects he felt strongly, such as the hypocrisy of the privileged and the suffering of the poor.[66] Nicknamed "the little wasp" because of his stinging attacks and sharp sense of humour, Jerrold's strong opinions, impatience, and intolerance frequently clashed with some of the other members. Thackeray was

FIGURE 2.2 "Authors' Miseries. No. VI." *Punch*, Vol. 15 (4 November 1848), p. 198.

Source: Punch, or The London Charivari

Jerrold's strongest opponent; while sympathetic to radical politics in his youth, Thackeray became increasingly conservative as he got older and more successful and had little patience for Jerrold's contempt for authority.[67] Jerrold, for his part, considered Thackeray a snob and "viewed his entrance into Society – against which Jerrold had for years been hurling his bitterest darts – with very grave suspicion."[68]

The men once sat next to one another at the weekly dinners but "there was as little love as space between them" and after his worldwide success with *Vanity Fair*, Thackeray resigned although he continued to maintain contact with the *Punch* men and occasionally joined them for the weekly dinner.[69] Although much has been made of the rivalry between Thackeray and Jerrold, theirs was a complex relationship that mixed animosity as well as support for each other.

On one occasion, Thackeray came especially into London from his lecturing tour to support Jerrold's election at the Reform Club. Thackeray was said to have exclaimed with delight, "We've got the little man in!" when the results were known. As he was an artist as well as writer for *Punch*, he once depicted himself next to Jerrold listening to passengers decrying the magazine (Figure 2.2).[70]

Another early departure due to a personality class with Jerrold was Albert Smith. Smith was a good friend of John Leech and Percival Leigh, a friendship that began when all three were young medical students at St. Bartholomew's Hospital. Smith was outgoing and informal and some attributed this to a "vulgar and bumptious" personality who "never neglected an opportunity for self-advertisement."[71] Both Thackeray and Jerrold disliked him intensely but only Jerrold showed his aversion to Smith directly and some accounts give Jerrold's relentless hostility as the reason for Smith's eventual resignation in 1843. Others claim that Smith's habit of showing *Punch* proofs to all at the Cheshire Cheese public house incurred Lemon's wrath that led to his dismissal. Regardless, Smith himself was both hurt and ignorant as to the reason for his alienation from the *Punch* group although this estrangement came to an end when he made a name for himself as an entertainer in his enormously popular "Mont Blanc" shows.[72]

By the end of the 1840s, Jerrold's radicalism was tempered within the pages of the magazine. Writing to his good friend Charles Dickens, Jerrold complained at the changing politics of the magazine,

> I do not very cordially agree with [*Punch*'s] new spirit. I am convinced that the world will get tired (at least I hope so) of this eternal guffaw at all things. After all, life has something serious in it. It cannot be all a comic history of humanity . . . . When, moreover, the change comes, unless *Punch* goes a little back to his occasional gravities, he'll be sure to suffer.[73]

In 1857, Jerrold was on his deathbed. The day before he died, he remembered his old friends and foes at *Punch* and sent a message to the Table through Ponny: "Tell the dear boys that if I've ever wounded any of them, I've always loved them."[74]

Years later in 1895, *Blackwood's Edinburgh Magazine* remembered Jerrold as "*Punch*'s evil genius" whose contributions, though brilliant, was "all tinctured with a rancorous and septic malignity."[75]

After Jerrold passed away, his memory continued to come up in conversation among the members, although the recollections were not always with fondness. Thackeray found an ally in Leech for they both shared a distaste for Jerrold and took turns verbally abusing the man while Lemon did his best to defend his deceased friend. Lemon determined that Thackeray's dislike for Jerrold was based on class prejudice, coinciding with Jerrold's accusations of snobbery. Silver records in his diary that Thackeray "said that DJ ate his peas with his knife and therefore was not fit company for him."[76]

Charterhouse-educated Silver was hired to replace Jerrold. A bashful and most obscure member, his greatest contribution to the legacy of *Punch* is his invaluable diary, which spans a twelve-year period from 1858 to 1870. Silver recorded conversations and tensions from the weekly dinners, which has allowed an intimate glimpse into the private space in which members of staff met, deliberated, discussed, and joked. Other contributors included Percival "the Professor" Leigh, "the mildest-mannered man that ever cut a throat – in argument."[77] He was good friends with Leech and Smith when the three were medical students and for decades, he provided the magazine with steady albeit unremarkable contributions. Leigh was a serious intellectual and after the death of his wife in 1847, he lived a quiet and eccentric lifestyle, enjoying his weekly dinners with the *Punch* men and they, in turn, enjoyed his storytelling at the Table.[78] Burnand remembers him fondly as "the dearest, kindest old boy, and a thorough gentleman in the truest and widest sense."[79] Leigh was so well liked that when his contributions became entirely useless, they would be re-written in order for them to appear in *Punch*, much to the old Professor's delight. Over time, however, his text could simply not be re-worked for publication but regardless, Leigh received an increase in salary to maintain him in old age.[80]

One of the first writers to join the magazine was Gilbert Abbott à Beckett, a shy and sagacious barrister who was also a Poor Law Commissioner and police magistrate.[81] He was an experienced editor and writer for the comic paper *Figaro in London* in the early 1830s before becoming *Punch*'s most reliable and prolific contributor, writing "regularly without a week's break until the day of his death, August 30, 1856."[82] Much like Burnand, à Beckett was said to be neutral in his political leanings; however, he sided with Thackeray in strongly recommending a heroic cartoon to welcome Louis-Napoléon Bonaparte's visit to Victoria and Albert in 1855. Both à Beckett and Thackeray believed that an alliance with France would best serve the interest of the British Empire but opposition at the Table was in favour of making a joke of this surprising visit. In the end, a compromise was reached and Bonaparte appeared in *Punch* ringing a visitor's bell of Buckingham Palace (Figure 2.3).[83]

FIGURE 2.3 "Who would have thought it?" *Punch*, Vol. 28 (21 April 1855), p. 155.

Source: Punch, or The London Charivari

Arthur à Beckett, Gilbert's son, also worked for *Punch* and was "credited with Tory bias."[84] Reflecting on his father's time at the magazine in its early years, Arthur categorised members of staff politically,

> Jerrold represented the extreme left, and Thackeray the most pronounced right. Mark Lemon – the best of editors – was neutral, with a tendency to Radicalism. My father, especially after he had been appointed a Metropolitan Police Magistrate, was also neutral, with a tendency to follow the policy of the *Times*.[85]

Arthur was correct in his placement of Jerrold and Thackeray in binary political opposition; Thackeray's conservatism was a constant antagonist to Jerrold's radicalism. Even Jerrold's perspective on Queen Victoria must have provoked Thackeray and others at the Table as Jerrold was one of her unequivocal and outspoken critics.[86] By the 1850s, however, the influence of Thackeray and his allies at *Punch* tempered Jerrold's radicalism and thus within only a decade of its founding, the political makeup of the magazine experienced a notable shift.

Edwin Milliken joined the Table in early 1877 after two years of being a regular contributor to *Punch*. His writings impressed Taylor, the editor at the time, who once asked him for a guarantee of the originality of his work. Spielmann describes Milliken's politics as "Radical" and he became known for his many verses devoted to honouring recently deceased and distinguished men, such as John Bright and Lord Tennyson, with much "generous sympathy." When public interest in China

FIGURE 2.4 "The British Lion's Vengeance on the Bengal Tiger" *Punch*, Vol. 33 (22 August 1857), pp. 76–77.

Source: Punch, or The London Charivari

increased during the closing years of the nineteenth century, Milliken was responsible for many of the verses and text that accompanied the cartoons representing foreign relations as well as the change in tone and attitude towards China and Japan. His literary post positioned Milliken as "the big drum . . . of the political orchestra."[87] The combination of his writings and the highly charged emotive cartoons worked together to reveal a heightened conscientiousness into Britain's intent on maintaining political and economic strength among imperial rivals.

The artists

Clever creativity

After Doyle's abrupt departure in 1850, Lemon found himself in a difficult position. He was in desperate need of an artist to illustrate the Pocket-book and Almanac that was due to come out. On the initiation of Jerrold, Lemon approached John Tenniel, who was initially indignant at being asked to join the magazine as a satirical artist. Tenniel was a classically trained painter and illustrator and he considered himself a true artist, above the "fooling" of cartoons. He asked a friend of his, "Do they suppose . . . that there is anything funny about *me*?"[88] He did ultimately join as a staff member and became good friends with John Leech during their time working together. In time, Tenniel eventually took over the Large Cuts from Leech who made known that he "detests big cutting" and in 1862, Tenniel became the chief (and most prolific) political artist and continued in this role for nearly forty years.[89]

In 1893, Tenniel became the first artist knighted for his work done mostly in black and white and eight years later, two hundred of Britain's most prominent men gathered in his honour to celebrate his retirement at the luxurious Hôtel Métropole in the West End. Tenniel claimed to care little for politics, "As for political opinions, I have none; at least, if I have my own little politics, I keep them to myself, and profess only those of my paper."[90] This lack of interest in politics is repeated by many of the *Punch* men, an odd assertion for those creating weekly political commentaries. In Tenniel's case, he was the most revered political cartoonist in the late nineteenth century, visually commenting on contentious political issues and it was his work that crystalised national and imperialist sentiments into easily comprehensible and attractive illustrations.

From 1841 to 1894, there were a total of 2,750 cartoons and Tenniel was the most prolific artist during this period, as demonstrated in the artist contribution table (Table 2.1).

TABLE 2.1 *Punch* Artist Contributions[91]

Sir John Tenniel	1,860
John Leech	720
Richard Doyle	70
Other Cartoonists	100
	2,750

Contrary to his statement of political neutrality, Tenniel's most powerful cartoons dealt directly with politics. For example, his 1857 "The British Lion's Vengeance on the Bengal Tiger" (Figure 2.4) is said to have effectively capture the nation's indignation over the rebellion of native Indian troops and the subsequent massacre at Cawnpore. A few months later, the *Illustrated London News* declared that "Mr. Tenniel's reputation stands too high to need eulogy, and the noble engraving which he supplied to *Punch* a few months ago, depicting the 'British Lion's Vengeance,' is in every household."[92]

Tenniel used dehumanising characteristics and grotesque distortions to mock anyone threatening social norms and hierarchies or British (specifically English) power and position at home and abroad. His cartoons appealed to a certain segment of Victorian society, namely, the conservative middle class, and Tenniel's intention was to trigger a chuckle, if only occasionally, at the expense of members of the lower classes and other suspects challenging the status quo. He complained that some people declared him too severe or dignified to be funny, but, he says, his "drawings are sometimes grotesque, but that is from a sense of fun and humour" and that he believed himself to have "a very keen sense of humour, and that [his] drawings are sometimes really funny!"[93]

Before Tenniel was chief cartoonist, that position was occupied by one of Thackeray's long-time friends and allies at *Punch*, the artist John Leech. Leech was a handsome and quiet individual who shared Thackeray's dislike of Jerrold but while Jerrold's powerful writing skills set the tone of the magazine, it was Leech who first defined the look with his highly popular illustrations. Thackeray once compared the two men, stating that Jerrold "looked up at the rich and great with a fierce, a sarcastic aspect, and a threatening posture" while Leech "surveys society from the gentleman's point of view."[94] Fellow artist George Du Maurier went further in describing Leech, stating,

> He was John Bull himself, but John Bull refined and civilized – John Bull polite, modest, gentle, full of self-respect and self-restraint; and with all the bully softened out of him; manly first and gentlemanly after, but very soon after; more at home perhaps in the club, the drawing-room, and the hunting-field, in Piccadilly and the Park, than in the farm or shop or market-place; a normal Englishman of the upper middle class.[95]

Leech delighted in a simple life; he loved children and horses and once proclaimed that his "tastes are very simple. Give me a good day's hunting, and some claret after it – nothing can be simpler, and I'm really quite contented."[96]

Leech suffered from bouts of melancholy and detested noise, enjoying nothing more than spending time in a quiet English seaside. He held a vehement hatred towards street musicians, in particular Italian organ grinders. Burnand remembers Leech thanking him for writing an article against street noises and Leech himself, as early as 1843, began his campaign against them in *Punch*.[97] In 1864, he died from angina pectoris;[98] Spielmann attributes the effects that noise emanating from Leech's despised organ grinders had on his serious heart condition and nervous affliction by "grinding his overworked nerves" until they "literally play[ed] him into his grave."[99]

Although Silver and Burnand recorded that normally, Leech showed no interest in politics and cared not to engage with political debates and conversation, he was a Tory who openly "sneer[ed] at the Working Man."[100] He also openly despised foreigners; so much so, that when Du Maurier was introduced to Leech for the first time, he was anxious that he would be mistaken as a foreigner on account of his name and went "out of [his] way to assure [Leech] that [he] was rather more English than John Bull himself."[101] These prejudices were dismissed by Thackeray, who commented, "These are lamentable prejudices, indeed; but what man is without his own?"[102] This indulgence towards Leech was maintained by the editors and proprietors of the magazine. When Leech angrily left the room on one occasion, Lemon commented that the artist had "always been a spoilt child."[103] The significance of Leech's contribution was so much so that Thackeray once claimed, "Leech *was Punch*" to which great offence was taken as his statement suggested the redundancy of the writers.[104] Despite provoking the ire of the writers, Thackeray was right to note Leech's importance for his cartoons were enormously popular with the public.[105] When he died, his illustrations continued to be admired and valued. An auction of his work at Christie's in April 1865 to raise money for Leech's widow and children generated £7,000 with buyers including William Gladstone.[106]

Du Maurier was brought to the Table after Leech's death. He was born in Paris and studied for a scientific career in chemistry, for which he was called a "shocking bad chemist." He was, however, a very talented artist but had little hopes for success as he was blind in one eye from a laboratory accident.[107] Silver remembered Du Maurier's introduction to the *Punch* staff when he made everyone uncomfortable by referring to his blindness.[108] Over time, Du Maurier became known and appreciated for his illustrations mocking society, manners, and etiquettes. This did not mean that he refrained from joining society, rather, his chronicles stemmed from his observations. Walter Besant persuaded Du Maurier to join the Rabelais Club which held literary dinners with its high-profile members including Thomas Hardy, Bret Harte, and Henry James.[109]

James noted that although Du Maurier was a great lover and illustrator of beauty, he also had "an artistic aesthetic need to make ugly people as ugly as they are" as he "finds a real entertainment in the completeness, in the perfection, of certain forms of facial queerness."[110] What was strange to Du Maurier was depicted as grotesques and fantastical figures, he had a "peculiar perception of the look of breeding, of race"[111] and was especially fond of ridiculing the awkward or out-of-place. For the men working at *Punch*, it was the lower classes, the Irish, the Jews, and anything – or anyone foreign that represented those who did not belong.[112]

Du Maurier also took a keen interest in theories of race and hereditary[113] and engaged with discourses of degeneration, targeting elements believed to contribute to the decline of the human, specifically the British, race such as disruptions of established class, racial, and gender hierarchies. From 1874 to 1882, Du Maurier created a series of cartoons in *Punch* lampooning participants of the New Aesthetic movement. These underscored ideas of degeneracy in morals as well as

FIGURE 2.5 "Ye Aesthetic Young Geniuses" *Punch*, Vol. 75 (21 September 1878), p. 122.

Source: Punch, or The London Charivari

physiognomy through his depictions of lacklustre and effeminate men (e.g. Figure 2.5). He would later explore these concepts in further detail in his successful novel *Trilby*, where he created the infamous figure of Svengali to represent racial degeneracy through "Jewishness."[114]

During the *Punch* dinners, Du Maurier sat next to his friend and fellow artist Charles Keene, who was a regular contributor for nine years before being invited to the Table in 1860. James describes Keene as being "English" and by way of explanation, he asserts that "half his jokes are against Scotchmen."[115] Keene was also extremely shy, detesting public appearances, and even among his colleagues at *Punch*, he was not a great conversationalist. He was known to puff silently on his pipe, listening to the discussion surrounding him and from time to time, softly chuckle to himself. Burnand declared Keene a great storyteller and "simply inimitable" when he was in the mood to explain his quiet mirth remembering occasions when the *Punch* men "cried with laughing" at one of his jokes.[116] Keene proposed very little and did not participate in suggestions for political cartoons; he only gave his opinion when asked and was apt to be negative or discouraging on projects under discussion. When pressed, Keene would likely pass criticism such as "D- – -d bad" before settling back into silence with his pipe.[117] Although he did not participate in proposing themes for the popular political cartoons, Keene was a self-proclaimed "hot Tory" who felt "so strongly antipathetic" towards Liberal tendencies that he kept his distance from *Punch* members whose political leanings he determined were too radical.[118]

Another artist, Edward Linley Sambourne, was invited to take a seat at the Table in 1871 although he was a regular contributor for years beforehand. His first drawing made its appearance on 27 April 1867 and was a decorated initial letter "T"; after which, Sambourne's works consisted primarily of initial letters and vignettes.[119] This changed over time when he was asked to provide a great variety of illustrations. However, he found the task of cartooning for the magazine daunting; in little over thirty-six hours following the weekly Wednesday dinners, the

FIGURE 2.6 "East and West" *Punch*, Vol. 119 (10 October 1900), p. 257.

Source: Punch, or The London Charivari

artists at *Punch* were expected to complete their artwork on Friday for submission to the engravers.[120]

Sambourne was particular about the accuracy of his depictions and in order to achieve his desired results, he needed both time and models to create his illustrations. In order to achieve this, Sambourne made extensive use of photographs, purchasing images from specialist dealers in shops around London as well as engaging his extended family and household staff in both taking and posing for photographs.[121] Unlike his contemporaries, he had little artistic training but he was viewed as a promising artist and was hired to assist *Punch*'s senior draughtsmen, Tenniel, Du Maurier, and Keene.[122] Sambourne was attuned to the magazine's hierarchy and most of the political subjects for his weekly cartoons were left for other members of staff to decide.[123] His diary is replete with notations on the subject of the cut assigned to him; for example, on Wednesday, 3 October 1900, Sambourne specified he "Got cut of German Emperor & China" to which he spent most of the following day completing the task with photographic assistance (see Figure 2.6).[124]

While Sambourne's need to accurately depict his subjects was of paramount concern, his colleague at *Punch*, Harry Furniss, lamented the ways in which the "wings of the caricaturist have been clipped." In 1894, he wrote:

> We don't caricature nowadays as the old caricaturists did; if we did, I don't know what pains and penalties we should court. Caricaturing in the savage, bitter sense has been killed more or less by the development of art . . . John Leech, as an unknown man, would not now get one of his drawings accepted by an editor. No one admires John Leech more than I do, and in the sense of humour and caricature, his work was perfect. But since Leech things have altered very much.[125]

Furniss, identified as a caricaturist of the previous generation when the works of James Gillray and Thomas Rowlandson dominated the satirical scene. To him, his co-artists at the magazine, such as Leech, Tenniel, and Sambourne, ushered in a sanitisation of caricatures for which he wholeheartedly disagreed.

Furniss complained,an honest satirist has no chance nowadays. He must not draw what he sees, or write what he really thinks about it. Pleasing wishy-washiness is idolised, whilst Hogarth is voted coarse. Great Scott! How this age of cigarettes and lemon squash would have stirred the pulse and nerved the brush of the greatest of English caricaturists![126]

Some of his caricatures did indeed cause offence; Spielmann notes, "wives would at times protest against the caricatures of husbands' figures, clothes, or faces" and Furniss's old classmate George Bernard Shaw wrote his "repulsive and unsympathetic caricatures of working-class humanity" overstepped "the line between ridicule and insult."[127] Furniss was born in Ireland to a Yorkshire father and Scottish mother and although he spent the first nineteen years of his life in Ireland, he downplayed this association. He was staunchly Unionist, emphatically anglophile, somewhat abrasive, and firmly against the women suffrage movement.[128]

Bernard Partridge joined the *Punch* Table in 1892, although his first artistic contribution to the magazine was the previous year. He was the son of a teacher of anatomy at the Royal Academy Schools and was known for his love of the stage. His art was much admired by Du Maurier, as both he and Partridge shared an appreciation of all that is beautiful.[129] Henry James claimed, "There is nothing, or almost nothing, of the horrible in *Punch*" and that English life is portrayed in the magazine through "several very wholesome tastes: the love of the country, the love of action, the love of a harmless joke within the limits of due reverence, the love of sport, of horses and dogs, of family life, of children, of horticulture."[130] This sanitation of humour must have annoyed the offensive-seeking Furniss.

The divergent personalities and outlooks among the *Punch* men resulted in an eclectic mix of social and political opinions and attitudes. Friendships formed and animosities simmered during the famous Wednesday dinners and yet at the end of every week, the oppositional perspectives managed to come together in order to create visual and textual commentaries for the magazine. The ability of several men of strong political persuasions and outlooks putting aside their clashes of opinion in order to produce a weekly political paper was essential for *Punch* to survive. Richard Altick explains that what is miraculous is that "an oddly assorted group of talented men managed to suppress whatever personal antipathies and frictions existed among them . . . in the interests of turning out, each week, a paper with a pronounced and distinctive flavour."[131] Editors played a key role in influencing the tone and character of the magazine, as discourses were re-oriented to suit their own political leanings. What remained consistent, however, was the sanitised humour that appealed to bourgeois sensibilities as well as *Punch*'s sense of nationalism and imperialism, all of which found expression in the text and visuals that will be discussed in more detail in the following sections.

Notes

1 Altick, *Punch*, p. XVII.
2 Spielmann, *The History of "Punch,"* p. 24.
3 Mr. Punch was a marionette in the eighteenth century and then transformed into a glove puppet at the opening of the nineteenth century. It was at this time that Mr. Punch became violent, which differed from the previous entertainment. Rosalind Crone, "Mr. and Mrs. Punch in Nineteenth-Century England" *The Historical Journal*, Vol. 49, No. 4 (December 2006), pp. 1055–1082; Alan Reeve and Martin Reeve, "Punch and Judy at the Beach and in the Mall" *Visual Culture in Britain*, Vol. 12, No. 1 (2011), p. 17. A showman complains that when he performs Punch and Judy shows for "sentimental folk," he must "leave out all comic words and business" as they will "have no ghost, no coffin, and no devil." Recorded in Henry Mayhew, *London Labour & the London Poor*, edited by Robert Douglas-Fairhurst (Oxford: Oxford University Press, 2010), pp. 240–241.
4 Leary, *The Punch Brotherhood*, p. 13.
5 Spielmann, *The History of "Punch,"* pp. 24–25.

6 Patrick Leary notes that "tree" was early Victorian slang for "table" although he states that he has been unable to find evidence to support this notion repeated by scholars. This reference is also made by Altick, *Punch*, footnote on p. 41, in which he states that "'Tree' was a colloquial word for dining table." For the call to attention, see "About" *Punch Magazine Cartoon Archive*. Online: https://www.punch.co.uk/about/index; for the caption, see Leary, *The Punch Brotherhood*, p. 18, footnote.
7 Leary, *The Punch Brotherhood*, p. 13.
8 Leary, *The Punch Brotherhood*, pp. 149–150.
9 Spielmann, *The History of "Punch,"* p. 272.
10 Spielmann, *The History of "Punch,"* pp. 33–35.
11 Leary, *The Punch Brotherhood*, for a discussion on Coyne, see p. 18; Mayhew's departure, see pp. 19–21; for Landells' negotiation process with Bradbury and Evans, see pp. 140–144.
12 Spielmann, *The History of "Punch,"* p. 257.
13 Altick, *Punch*, p. 42.
14 Athol Mayhew, *A Jorum of "Punch,"* (London: Downey & Co., 1895), p. 109.
15 Banta, *Barbaric Intercourse*, p. 23.
16 Spielmann, *The History of "Punch,"* p. 392.
17 Spielmann notes that in the United Kingdom, it was standard practice in journals and periodicals that contributors sending in jokes seek "neither pay nor recognition." See Spielmann, *The History of "Punch,"* p. 139.
18 Henry Silver, 23 July 1862, Henry Silver Diary, *Punch* Archive, British Library.
19 George Somes Layard, *Shirley Brooks of "Punch," His Life, Letters and Diaries* (New York: H. Holt and Company, 1907), p. 117.
20 Spielmann, *The History of "Punch,"* p. 266.
21 Spielmann, *The History of "Punch,"* p. 263.
22 Leary, *The Punch Brotherhood*, p. 51.
23 Altick, *Punch*, p. XIX.
24 Leary, *The Punch Brotherhood*, p. 124.
25 Spielmann, *The History of "Punch,"* p. 356.
26 *The Man in the Moon* was a monthly periodical started by the ex-staff member Albert Smith as a direct competition to *Punch*.
27 Leary, *The Punch Brotherhood*, pp. 111, 114.
28 Layard, *Shirley Brooks of "Punch,"* p. 116.
29 Leary, *The Punch Brotherhood*, p. 126.
30 Spielmann, *The History of "Punch,"* p. 359.
31 Layard, *Shirley Brooks*, p. 117.
32 Leary, *The Punch Brotherhood*, p. 131.
33 Leary, *The Punch Brotherhood*, p. 121. On Lemon's concern, p. 119.
34 Silver, 21 March 1860, Henry Silver Diary.
35 Silver, 2 March 1859, Henry Silver Diary; Spielmann, *The History of "Punch,"* p. 71.
36 Leary, *The Punch Brotherhood*, p. 51.
37 K. G. Robbins, "Public Opinion, the Press and Pressure Groups" *British Foreign Policy under Sir Edward Grey* (ed.) F. H. Hinsley (Cambridge: Cambridge University Press, 1977), p. 80 cited in David Brown, "Diplomacy and the Fourth Estate: The Role of the Press in British Foreign Policy in the Age of Palmerston" *On the Fringes of Diplomacy: Influences on British Foreign Policy, 1800–1945* (eds.) John Fisher and Antony Best (Farnham; Burlington, VT: Ashgate Publishing Co., 2011), p. 39.
38 Spielmann, *The History of "Punch,"* p. 99.
39 Spielmann, *The History of "Punch,"* p. 340.
40 Shearer West, "Tom Taylor, William Powell Frith, and the British School of Art" *Victorian Studies*, Vol. 33, No. 2 (Winter 1990), p. 308; Leary, *The Punch Brotherhood*, pp. 22–23.
41 Spielmann, *The History of 'Punch,'* p. 362; See also footnote, Leary, *The Punch Brotherhood*, p. 32.

42 Spielmann, *The History of "Punch,"* p. 151.
43 Spielmann, *The History of "Punch,"* p. 80.
44 Spielmann, *The History of "Punch,"* p. 367.
45 "The Death of Sir Frances Burnand" *Evening Mail*, Monday 23 April 1917, p. 8.
46 Philip Waller, "Roman Candles" *Politics and Culture in Victorian Britain* (eds.) Peter Ghosh and Lawrence Goldman (Oxford: Oxford University Press, 2006), p. 210.
47 Doyle was also unreliable in producing illustrations in a timely manner. See Leary, *The Punch Brotherhood*, p. 157; for *Punch* and anti-Catholic sentiments, see McNees, "'Punch' and the Pope," pp. 18–45.
48 Spielmann, *The History of "Punch,"* p. 363.
49 Francis Burnand, *Records and Reminiscences, Personal and General*, Vol. II (London: Methuen & Co., 1904), p. 228.
50 Layard, *Shirley Brooks*, p. 116.
51 Leary, *The Punch Brotherhood*, p. 18.
52 Spielmann, *The History of "Punch,"* p. 74.
53 Silver, 23 July 1862, Henry Silver Diary.
54 Spielmann, *The History of "Punch,"* p. 25.
55 Spielmann, *The History of 'Punch,'* p. 74; Leary, *The Punch Brotherhood*, p. 12.
56 Burnand, *Records and Reminiscences*, p. 12.
57 Altick, *Punch*, p. 125.
58 Leary, *The Punch Brotherhood*, p. 23 referring to "John Bull Beaten" *Punch*, Vol. 20, p. 115; Spielmann, *The History of "Punch,"* pp. 456–457.
59 Spielmann, *The History of "Punch,"* pp. 272–273, 436–437.
60 Leary, *The Punch Brotherhood*, p. 7.
61 Altick, *Punch*, pp. 44–45.
62 Spielmann, *The History of "Punch,"* p. 101.
63 Leary, *The Punch Brotherhood*, p. 159.
64 Burnand, *Records and Reminiscences*, Vol. II, p. 8.
65 Spielmann, *The History of "Punch,"* p. 287.
66 Walter Jerrold, *Douglas Jerrold and "Punch"* (London: Macmillan and Co., Limited, 1910), p. 12.
67 Leary, *The Punch Brotherhood*, pp. 24–25.
68 Spielmann, *The History of "Punch,"* p. 74.
69 Spielmann, *The History of "Punch,"* p. 74; Leary, *The Punch Brotherhood*, p. 25.
70 Spielmann, *The History of "Punch,"* pp. 311–312; Jerrold's grandson Walter disagreed that there was animosity and bad feelings between Douglas and Thackeray. He expresses his doubt in his *Douglas Jerrold and "Punch,"* pp. 26–33.
71 Spielmann, *The History of "Punch,"* pp. 303–306.
72 Spielmann, *The History of "Punch,"* p. 304; Leary, *The Punch Brotherhood*, p. 19.
73 Blanchard Jerrold, *The Life and Remains of Douglas Jerrold* (Boston: Ticknor and Fields, 1859), p. 249.
74 Spielmann, *The History of 'Punch,'* p. 297.
75 J. H. Millar, "The Life of 'Punch' *Blackwood's Edinburgh Magazine*, December 1895, p. 870.
76 Cited in Leary, *The Punch Brotherhood*, pp. 30–31.
77 Spielmann, *The History of "Punch,"* p. 71.
78 Leary, *The Punch Brotherhood*, p. 22.
79 Burnand, *Records and Reminiscences*, p. 17.
80 Spielmann, *The History of "Punch,"* pp. 302–303.
81 Leary, *The Punch Brotherhood*, p. 21.
82 Arthur à Beckett, *The à Becketts of "Punch"* (New York: E.P. Dutton and Co., 1903), pp. 23–28.
83 À Beckett, *The à Becketts of "Punch,"* pp. 65–67.
84 Spielmann, *The History of "Punch,"* p. 80.

85 À Beckett, *The à Becketts of "Punch,"* pp. 64–65.
86 Altick, *Punch*, pp. 17–18.
87 Spielmann, *The History of "Punch,"* pp. 80, 377–378.
88 Spielmann, *The History of "Punch,"* p. 466.
89 Silver, 17 February 1859, Henry Silver Diary. *Punch* Archive. British Library.
90 Spielmann, *The History of "Punch,"* p. 463.
91 Spielmann, *The History of "Punch,"* p. 172.
92 *Illustrated London News*, 16 January 1858, p. 70.
93 Spielmann, *The History of ' "Punch,"* p. 463.
94 Spielmann, *The History of "Punch,"* p. 421.
95 George Du Maurier, *Social Pictorial Satire: Reminiscences and Appreciations of English Illustrators of the Past Generation* (New York; London: Harper & Brothers Publishers, 1898), p. 21.
96 Altick, *Punch*, p. 71.
97 Burnand, *Records and Reminiscences*, pp. 9–10.
98 Du Maurier, *Social Pictorial Satire*, p. 19.
99 Spielmann, *The History of "Punch,"* p. 437; Du Maurier also notes Leech's hatred of noise and buskers, see Du Maurier, *Social Pictorial Satire*, pp. 40–41.
100 Silver cited in Layard, *Shirley Brooks of "Punch,"* pp. 115–116; Burnand, *Records and Reminiscences*, p. 10; Silver Diary, 11 April 1864 cited in Leary, *The Punch Brotherhood*, footnote on p. 24.
101 Du Maurier, *Social Pictorial Satire*, p. 9. On Leech hating foreigners, see p. 13 and again on p. 40.
102 Spielmann, *The History of "Punch,"* p. 437.
103 Leary, *The Punch Brotherhood*, p. 21.
104 Leary, *The Punch Brotherhood*, p. 33 and footnote number 87.
105 Spielmann, *The History of "Punch,"* p. 420.
106 Henry J. Miller, "John Leech and the Shaping of the Victorian Cartoon: The Context of Respectability" *Victorian Periodicals Review*, Vol. 42, No. 3 (Fall 2009), p. 267.
107 Spielmann, *The History of "Punch,"* pp. 503–504.
108 Layard, *Shirley Brooks*, p. 223.
109 Philip V. Allingham, "George du Maurier, Illustrator and Novelist" *The Victorian Web*, online: www.victorianweb.org/art/illustration/dumaurier/pva95.html.
110 Henry James, *Partial Portraits*, p. 348.
111 James, *Partial Portraits*, p. 350.
112 On *Punch* depictions of the strange and awkward, see Banta *Barbaric Intercourse*, Chapter 2 "Out of Place" with discussion on Du Maurier specifically found on pp. 76–90.
113 On Du Maurier depictions of the awkward, see Banta *Barbaric Intercourse*, pp. 76–77; on his interest in race and hereditary, see Spielmann, *The History of "Punch,"* p. 505.
114 Laura Vorachek, "Mesmerists and Other Meddler: Social Darwinism, Degeneration, and Eugenics in Trilby" *Victorian Literature and Culture*, Vol. 37, No. 1 (2009), p. 199.
115 James, *Partial Portraits*, p. 340.
116 Burnand, *Records and Reminiscences*, p. 10.
117 Layard, *The Life and Letters of Charles Samuel Keene of "Punch,"* p. 76.
118 Spielmann, *The History of "Punch,"* pp. 78, 481.
119 Leonée Ormond, "Edward Linley Sambourne: A Cartoonist in the Art World" *The British Art Journal*, Vol. 3, No. 1 (Autumn 2001), p. 5.
120 Reena Suleman, "Out of the Ordinary: Linley Sambourne and the Amateur Model" *The British Art Journal*, Vol. 3, No. 1 (Autumn 2001), p. 28.
121 Suleman, *Out of the Ordinary*, pp. 28–35.
122 Spielmann, *The History of "Punch,"* p. 532.
123 Scully and Varnava, "Introduction," p. 1.
124 Edward Linley Sambourne, 3 October 1900 and 4 October 1900, Edward Linley Sambourne Diary.

125 Cited in Gareth Cordery and Joseph Meisel (eds.), *The Humours of Parliament* (Columbus: Ohio State University Press, 2014), p. 7.
126 Cited in Cordery and Meisel (eds.), *The Humours of Parliament*, p. 7.
127 Spielmann, *The History of "Punch,"* p. 551. Bernard Shaw cited in Cordery and Meisel (eds.), *The Humours of Parliament*, p. 8.
128 Gareth Cordery, *An Edwardian's View of Dickens and His Illustrators* (Greensboro: University of North Carolina, ELT Press, 2005), pp. 1–2; Cordery and Meisel (eds.), *The Humours of Parliament*, p. 9.
129 Spielmann, *The History of "Punch,"* pp. 564–565.
130 James, *Partial Portraits*, pp. 336–337.
131 Altick, *Punch*, p. 42.

3

"PUNCH IS AN ENGLISH INSTITUTION"

The attitude of the magazine

On Tuesday, 22 June 1897, Linley Sambourne records events of Queen Victoria's Diamond Jubilee in his diary. He notes, "Her Majesty's most glorious 60th Jubilee Year of Reign" and with "Troops marching past," he "Saw the whole procession."[1] Victoria was seventy-eight years of age and at the time of her Diamond Jubilee, she had become a powerful symbol of imperial unity. Guests of honour included the eleven colonial Premiers, accompanied by their nation's military representing the entire British empire.[2] John Tenniel commemorated the event in "For Queen and Empire!" capturing the nationalistic and imperialistic fervour which the festivities celebrated in a double-page spread (Figure 3.1). Mr. Punch, the magazine's mascot, genuflects to Victoria, a gesture reflecting the deference generally held by the *Punch* men for their Queen.

Spielmann states the magazine "has shown unswerving chivalry and reverence" towards Victoria and "every important incident in the life of the Queen has been touched upon with the utmost respect and sympathy."[3] When Victoria was nearing the end of her life, Sambourne made note that "Her Majesty [was] slowly sinking" and expressed "Great anxiety." Upon her death, he was in a "Frightful rush all day & much worried" and witnessed the funeral from the corner of Pall Mall and St. James's Street, where he patiently waited "from 8.30 to 11.30 when her late Majesty's funeral procession passed."[4] Indeed, throughout the Queen's life, the artists at *Punch* refrained from depicting her as a grotesque figure with exaggerated features, a common technique cartoonists employ to lampoon their targets. Other public figures, however, were not given this same consideration; foreigners were frequent targets, including Victoria's German husband, Prince Albert, who was mercilessly ridiculed by the *Punch* staff, his unpopularity owing to the fact that he was of a "foreign nationality."[5]

DOI: 10.4324/9781003025573-3

FIGURE 3.1 "For Queen and Empire" *Punch*, Vol. 112 (19 June 1897), pp. 302–303.

Source: Punch, or The London Charivari

As discussed in the previous chapter, there was substantial prejudice against foreigners and in a period of heightened geopolitical awareness, imperial rivals portrayed in *Punch* were consistently depicted as tyrants or mutinous rebels if they threatened Britain's balance of power on the international arena. Spielmann asserted, "[f]rom first to last, *Punch* has always been an Imperialist"[6] as well as "an Englishman of intense patriotism."[7] This chapter explores the characteristic tone and "attitude" of the magazine. As members of staff became conscientious of its readership, so too were they aware of their respective roles in shaping the views of the British public. The chapter begins by taking a look at *Punch*'s move away from scurrility, the genre to which satirical journalism traditionally belonged. This was significant in establishing the magazine as a popular periodical that all members of the Victorian family could enjoy as the content coincided with notions of respectability.

The content also shifted from its initial radical stance to a more conservative outlook that promoted nationalistic and imperialistic sentiments. One of the most effective means of doing this was through their Large Cuts, or full page or double page cartoons, which were almost always political and an important feature that distinguished *Punch* from its predecessors of satirical periodicals. The ingenious format of the Large Cuts combined parodies, literary material, familiar childhood rhymes and tales, with cutting political commentaries and comical caricatures. John Tenniel and Linley Sambourne were central figures in creating the cartoons during this period. Tenniel's first contribution to the magazine appeared in 1851 and his last in 1901, resulting in a total of twenty-three hundred cartoons.[8] The focus of the final section of this chapter explores the ways in which these attractive visuals became significant conduits in the circulation and dissemination of cultural and political knowledge.

Mr. Punch

The gentleman imperialist

Except for a few interruptions, *Punch* ran for one hundred and sixty years[9] and is frequently referred to as a pillar of the Victorian middle-class establishment and a national institution as well as one of the most successful and influential comic magazines of the English-speaking world.[10] One of the main factors contributing to *Punch*'s early success was owed, as Richard Altick notes, "less to what it was at the outset of its career – which was nothing much – than to what it was not."[11] It is significant that Mark Lemon, as one of the founders and first editor of *Punch*, set the standard to which subsequent editors would follow. Lemon ensured that the magazine kept a safe distance from offensive jokes and this contrasted starkly with the tradition of comic periodicals that were notorious for their obscenity and scandalous articles along with images of wizened or grotesque figures in compromising positions. Instead, *Punch* was said to be "the personification of rousing merriment and honest, cleanly fun" that distinguished itself from previous mode of satire "which, under the guise of 'comic' journalism, wedded the badinage of the gutter to the bludgeon of the blackmailer."[12] "*Punch* keeps up," Lemon declared one evening, "by its keeping to the gentlemanly view of things"[13] and this approval of the magazine's clean and respectable sense of wit and humour was reiterated throughout the period.

Just one year after *Punch*'s inaugural issue in 1841, *The Times* was already endorsing the magazine and attributing its success to its sense of decency:

> There is one thing, in addition to the cleverness of *Punch*, which has not a little contributed to its success, and that is the unvarying good humour and propriety which prevail in it, and the total exclusion from its pages of all that is gross, low, or coarsely personal, a discipline the absence of which has swamped many previous attempts of the same kind.[14]

In 1842, the *Westminster Review*, one of the top journals aimed at an intellectual readership, published a fifty-three-page illustrated article on the first two volumes of *Punch*. This was remarkable; never before had a sophisticated journal given serious consideration to a magazine that was devoted to comical commentaries.[15]

The *Westminster Review*'s article was interspersed by woodcut illustrations, lent by the "the Proprietor," and the purpose was to evaluate *Punch*'s textual and visual contents. The conclusion was generally positive and attention was paid to the sanitation of humour that Lemon worked hard to maintain. It asserts:

> We have been justified in dwelling for awhile on this amusing periodical by several considerations. One its moral superiority to the publications with a similar aim by which it was preceded. The "Satirist," the "Age," the "John Bull," have endeavoured to avail themselves of the weapons of wit and humour, but their best puns rarely rise above the level of obscene jests, and none such disgrace the columns of "Punch."[16]

The article also makes note with "much satisfaction" the "clever" wood-cut illustrations which were deemed an "improvement in the art of wood engraving."[17]

Lemon's resolve that *Punch* should abide by Victorian rules of conduct and notions of respectability was a shrewd business decision. By changing the nature of satire in sanitising both textual and visual humour, *Punch* was not only set apart and stood out among its competitors, but it was also allowed to establish itself within the home of respectable Victorian families. Henry James wrote that *Punch* "has always been discreet, even delicate" and that the magazine has "rarely been guilty of a violation of decorum" thereby establishing *Punch* as a family magazine, which "may be sent up to the nursery."[18] *Punch* staff member William Thackeray also praised the magazine for its family-friendly sense of humour by claiming, "there never was before published in this world so many volumes that contained so much cause for laughing, and so little for blushing; so many jokes, and so little harm." He went further by stating, "We will laugh in the company of our wives and children; we will tolerate no indecorum; we like that our matrons and girls should be pure."[19]

Punch's sense of decency was an essential ingredient in contributing to the success of the magazine but what exactly was *Punch*'s humour? In the inaugural issue, "The Moral of Punch" considers it "best to be merry and wise" and quoting Lord Byron, "laugh at all things, for we wish to know, What, after all, are all the things but a show!"[20] Indeed, the magazine became famous for commenting on topical subjects in a seemingly jovial and good-natured manner; however, which topics were selected for comical commentary and how they were textually or visually represented reveals a highly ideological and political awareness. Despite assertions to the contrary, *Punch*'s humour was not always friendly nor was it harmless.

In one of his lectures on the art of England, John Ruskin describes the politics of *Punch* as follows:

> He is a polite Whig, with a sentimental respect for the Crown, and a practical respect for property. He steadily flatters Lord Palmerston, from his heart adores Mr. Gladstone; steadily, but not virulently, caricatures Mr. D'Israeli; violently and virulently castigates assault upon property, in any kind, and hold up for the general ideal of perfection, to be aimed at by all the children of heaven and earth, the British Hunting Squire, the British Colonel, and the British Sailor.[21]

After its initial radicalism subsided, *Punch*'s content and tone was tamed and the magazine's staff was satisfied with creating mild jabs at social foibles in hopes of eliciting chuckles from its primarily conservative middle-class readers.

Punch also became patriotic and imperialistic and both tone and content reflected these sentiments, at times with fervour. "The policy of *Punch*," Lemon declared, "is to ignore the fact that England has been humbled, if fact it be"[22] and true to these words, Lemon and staff members were conscientious of representing Britain as morally upright when depicted among the international community. By the 1890s, *Punch* created a magazine that firmly sided with Britain and its imperialist ambitions and used the popularity of its Large Cut cartoons to promote this agenda. If the aim of satire is to express moral conviction with concern for public interest, then the boundaries between "right" and "wrong" must be made clear.

"The Moral of Punch" claimed that the magazine's objective is to "Destroy the principle of evil by increasing the means of cultivating the good"[23] but as Martha Banta rightly points out, "whose 'right' and whose 'wrong' must [satire] choose, once it entangles itself in confusion over 'good' or 'bad' intercourse, driven by norms that rule the conduct accepted by the civilization of which it is very much a part?"[24] The following section examines *Punch*'s Large Cut cartoons, which were important vehicles in circulating and disseminating ideas on who, according to the magazine, was on the "right" side of history vis-à-vis wider geopolitical concerns. Through patterns of repetition and easily comprehensible tropes and figures, the cartoons provide a clear understanding of a larger narrative framework that includes wider concerns about foreign relations and Britain's position in the global community.

Mr. Punch's big cut

The Large Cut cartoons

In the 1840s, *Punch* artist John Leech coined the term "cartoon" to refer to satirical drawings and although the magazine dropped the word, it gained wide currency until eventually, it came to refer to any comical illustration.[25] *Punch*'s cartoons included illustrations interspersed around text, often called "social cuts," elaborate ornamental initials, as well as the full page images initially called "pencilling," and later, "big cuts" or "large cuts."[26] This combination of text and images provided a model for future comic magazines and revolutionised London's daily newspapers by integrating cartoons with political journalism.[27] *Punch*'s Large Cuts were another essential element in the magazine's success; the images were immensely popular and represented *Punch*'s public identity.[28] The word "cut" could not have been more apt. The magazine's cartoons with their razor-sharp humour often cut both ways and it can be difficult to discern exactly who was the target of the joke and who received sympathy. Furthermore, the word "cut" accurately reflects the broader environment in which these cartoons arose.

In order for a topic to make the cut, *Punch* staff members needed shrewd business acumen in order to survive the cut-throat world of the nineteenth century periodical press, which was highly competitive and volatile.[29] Only topics deemed "hot" enough in the press would merit a Large Cut. This ensured the cartoons would be comprehensible because the chosen topics would be at the forefront of public consciousness. The decision-making process occurred at the weekly Wednesday dinners, after the evening meal, when someone at the Table would suggest a subject and spark debates and arguments as the men, each with their own opinions and political leanings, jostled to have his idea accepted and made into a Large Cut.[30] The deciding factor was based on the popularity of the topic or event in leading daily news, in particular *The Times*. *Punch*'s partiality for *The Times* was well known and the magazine was often referred to as the visual accompaniment to the newspaper's textual commentaries. This preference was illustrated in 1846 with a small cartoon of two men reading the press: one enjoys *Punch* by the fireside while the other is engulfed in the news from *The Times* (Figure 3.2).

The daily press was essential for *Punch*'s existence; without the news, the magazine would have no material to satirise. The magazine also accepted contributions and as a popular publication, *Punch* inevitably attracted a host of hopefuls that varied in quality. Spielmann commented that the calibre of the jokes "is sufficient to prove how deficient in wit, if not in humour, is the English people considered as a community."[31] At times, the national practice of sending in jokes and illustrations proved fruitful for the editors as they search for new talent. Francis Burnand and Harry Furniss both sent in contributions before being invited as members of staff. The reliance on the news, however, came with challenges. In October 1871, Tenniel visualised frustration at not having any newsworthy source by depicting Mr. Punch kicking up various newspapers in vexation at the lack of notable subjects (Figure 3.3). Another problem was the danger in reiterating and circulating false news.

During the Boxer Uprising in China, *The Times* and *Daily Mail* reprinted an erroneous report that the British legations in Beijing had fallen to the Boxers and the entire foreign community was massacred. A memorial service was immediately planned for St. Paul's Cathedral[32] and Tenniel created an emotionally super-charged Large Cut titled, "The Avenger!" (Figure 3.4) depicting a winged warrior mounted on a white steed bearing down on a dragon, the symbol of China. The warrior, with the words "civilisation" inscribed on his wings, draws on connections readers may have with the familiar legend of England's patron saint, St. George. *Punch* frequently used familiar and well-loved stories, such as myths and legends, to render complicated topical subjects into easily legible images and to ensure readers' understanding of the message.

Themes of school children or caricatures set within a classroom to visualise politics were frequently employed. *Punch* also used familiar and instantly recognisable allegorical figures, such as Britannia and John Bull, and its cartoon versions became both popular and distinguishable. Tenniel, for example, refused to give into the pressure Brooks applied in attempting to convince him to "modernise" his depiction of John Bull and this meant that the figures remained both consistent and familiar to readers and over time, they became legendary.[33] Topics that may be too

FIGURE 3.2 "Untitled" *Punch*, Vol. 10 (14 March 1846), p. 114.

Source: Punch, or The London Charivari

obscure were avoided and if there were concerns that the cartoon might bewilder the observer, an accompanying poem or article was assigned for clarification and the text was equally important.

The careful attention paid to ensure the magazine's message was understood made the artists' job challenging. Not only were they required to be artistically talented in order to create attractive illustrations but they were also judged by their ability to disentangle the chaotic nature of the discussions at the Table in order to translate complex topics into simple and comprehensible cartoons. In 1863, Burnand wondered "how Tenniel gets the notion [for the Large Cut] out of such

"NOTHING IN THE PAPERS!"

FIGURE 3.3 "Nothing in the Papers!" *Punch*, Vol. 61 (21 October 1871), p. 167.

Source: Punch, or The London Charivari

a chaos of talk about it."[34] For Tenniel, he frequently expressed frustration at the verbal, and not visual, character of the discussions. On one occasion, he cried out in frustration, "How am I to draw posterity?"[35]

Leech was also cognisant of the importance of the imagined readers' understanding. He was said to "have cared little about politics" and rarely joined in the debates and discussions around the Table, only voicing his opinion if he was unable to visualise the proposed topic.[36] In February 1859, Brooks suggested that the Large Cut should comment on Napoleon III's aggressive policies on the Continent."You can *draw* a sword, you know, Leech" – sitting on a powder barrel and smoking the pipe of peace. "Yes, that's easy enough," says Leech, "but how can people know that it *is* the pipe of peace, unless I put a label on it, and that would look ridiculous?"[37] In the end, Leech created "The French Porcupine" bristling with bayonets while simultaneously declaring "*L'Empire, c'est la paix*" (the Empire is the peace), a clear visual message of France's hostile intentions (Figure 3.5).

One of the most clever techniques *Punch* was highly skilled at employing was the double topicality cartoon, which combined two current events into a single Large Cut. In 1869 when the Siamese Twins, Chang and Eng, were scheduled to appear at the Egyptian Hall in London, Tenniel depicted the Church of England and the Church of Ireland conjoined with Gladstone ready to separate them with the blade of "Disestablishment'" (Figure 3.6). The cartoons combined

FIGURE 3.4 "The Avenger!" *Punch*, Vol. 119 (25 July 1900), pp. 64–65.

Source: Punch, or The London Charivari

FIGURE 3.5 "The French Porcupine" *Punch*, Vol. 36 (19 February 1859), p. 75.

Source: Punch, or The London Charivari

political news with a popular non-political event to give readers two of-the-moment events in the most *Punch*iest of cuts.[38] In another cartoon titled, "In the Movement" (Figure 3.7), the cartoon used double topicality to comment on two political events. In this cartoon, the Empress Dowager Cixi pushes her belongings on a flat wheelbarrow as she moves capitals. Paul Krüger, the President of the South African Republic and representative of the Boer cause, peeps at Cixi over a wall and mutters to himself, "Shifting her capital? My idea!" In 1900, the Eight-Nation Alliance reached the capital and brought an end to the Court supported Boxer Uprising; the same year, Krüger left the Transvaal in exile after his defeat in the Boer War.

The double-topicality cartoons only worked if both topics featured prominently in the newspapers and many topics were selected simply because they were the most talked-about subjects in London. When the news about Abraham Lincoln's assassination reached London, it was agreed among the *Punch* men that this was too big an event to not merit a Large Cut. Brooks was not present that Wednesday evening but Tom Taylor suggested a cut showing a sorrowful Britannia placing a wreath over a funeral bier (Figure 3.8). Tenniel created the cut, Lemon added the caption, and Taylor wrote accompanying verses.[39] When Brooks returned the following week, he was upset by Taylor's text, arguing that the verses placed the magazine in a bad light as *Punch* was previously critical of Lincoln and the North during the American Civil War. "*Punch* can do no wrong," Brooks furiously declared.[40]

FIGURE 3.6 "Our Siamese Twins" *Punch*, Vol. 56 (13 February 1869), p. 59.

Source: Punch, or The London Charivari

IN THE MOVEMENT.

OOM PAUL (*to himself*). "SHIFTING HER CAPITAL? MY IDEA!"

FIGURE 3.7 "In the Movement" *Punch*, Vol. 119 (29 August 1900), p. 155.

Source: Punch, or The London Charivari

Although both Lemon and Henry Silver disagreed with Brooks, the Large Cuts tended to appeal to nationalist sentiments. Tenniel's 1857 "The British Lion's Vengeance on the Bengal Tiger" (see the previous chapter, Figure 2.4) is powerfully evocative in its portrayal of the lion pouncing upon the tiger in defence of a helpless woman and child under attack. Upon publication, Silver noted in his diary that this cartoon "increased the circulation"[41] and indeed, Tenniel's cartoons were extremely popular. The *Daily Telegraph* reported, "the world awaited the advent of his cartoon at the judgment seat"[42] and what was being judged was usually a political subject, sometimes fiercely contested among the *Punch* men. With diverging political opinions between them, divisive topics and unsettling questions were unsurprisingly the cause of much heated debate at the Table.

One such argument occurred over the contentious issue of Governor Eyre, who brutally suppressed a slave rebellion in Jamaica and was brought to trial in England. In writing about the trial, Charles L. Graves declared that *Punch* "never swerved from the firm conviction that [Eyre] had saved Jamaican society, white and black, by his promptness and resolution."[43] In reality, the issue was divisive.

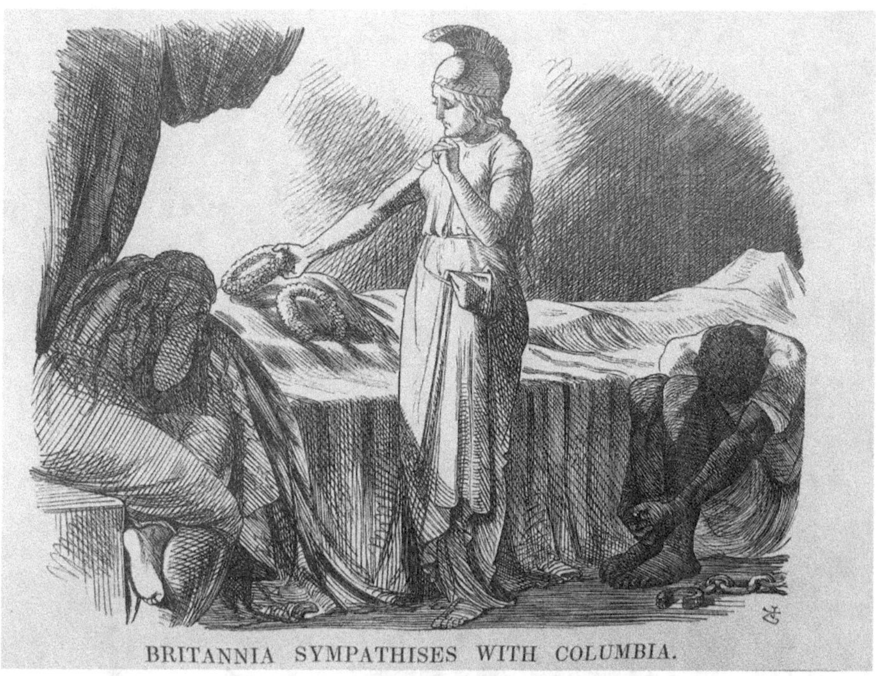

FIGURE 3.8 "Britannia Sympathises with Columbia" *Punch*, Vol. 48 (6 May 1865), p. 183.

Source: Punch, or The London Charivari

Lemon, Brooks, Leigh, and Mayhew wanted a Large Cut defending Eyre whereas Silver and Taylor disagreed with Taylor stating that he would "have no hand in the Cut."[44] Silver and Taylor's dissenting voices were the minority and at the end of the controversy in May 1868, Leigh clearly positioned the magazine's defence for Eyre for its readers:

> Ye savages thirsting for bloodshed and plunder,
> Ye miscreants burning for rapine and prey,
> By the fear of the lash and the gallows kept under,
> Henceforth who shall venture to stand in your way?
> Run riot, destroy, ravage, kill without pity,
> Let any man how he molests you beware,
> Behold how hard the Jamaica Committee,
> To ruin are trying to hunt gallant Eyre.[45]

Whatever the differences of political opinion among the *Punch* men, they were generally clear about the class and race they were engaging with, whether mocking or bonding, especially after the death of Jerrold and his radical political outlook.

FIGURE 3.9 "The Rhodes Colossus" *Punch*, Vol. 103 (10 December 1892), p. 266.

Source: Punch, or The London Charivari

FIGURE 3.10 "The Triumph of Civilisation!" *Punch*, Vol. 107 (11 August 1894), p. 62.

Source: Punch, or The London Charivari

Large Cuts of empire expansion increased substantially during this period of heightened imperial identity and geopolitical competition. Sambourne's "The Rhodes Colossus" provides a good example (Figure 3.9) as it was an incredible success at the time and continues to be an enduring visible representation of British imperialism. In 1895, *Blackwood's Edinburgh Magazine* praised it as a "triumph of bold perspective."[46] The cartoon signified Britain bringing progress and modernity to the African continent and thus the image, along with *Punch*'s various Large Cuts dealing with imperialism, shaped understandings of empire and "otherness" in the British imagination.[47] The subject matters in *Punch* were continually commended for its ability to accurately reflect the "public spirit" and Sambourne's 1892 depiction of Cecil Rhodes was published at a time of increased imperialist fervour. *Punch*'s Large Cuts provided British readers with a means of engaging with empire as well as issues of imperialism and due to the careful attention paid to illustrate the most newsworthy events, these images reveal what was being discussed at a particular point in time.

This did not mean, however, that *Punch* refrained from criticising aspects of Britain's engagement with foreign nations. The magazine was consistently critical of aggressive foreign trade framed under the rhetoric of civilisation. In 1894, at the beginning of open hostilities in the First Sino-Japanese war, Sambourne illustrated the perceived result of "exporting civilisation" by depicting the allegorical figure, "Civilisation" standing among an arsenal of modern weaponry as she observes two Asian dragons in the midst of a vicious combat (Figure 3.10). She watches and "cries,/'Is this *my* work?'" Burnand wrote the accompanying verses and asks "what has the West taught to the East,/Save the science of war, and tippling?" The East were not beyond reproach; China and Japan were eager to receive and use weapons against each other, taking "from the White-man all that's bad" and welcoming "Big Guns" while vigorously rejecting the teachings of the Bible.[48]

Sambourne's Large Cut and Burnand's accompanying verses challenge Britain's civilising mission abroad. They prompt questions about the nature of relations with foreign nations and how to engage with people outside British society and behavioural frameworks. In *Punch*'s inaugural issue, the Botecudo is illustrated "disfigured by civilisation," the unfortunate result of one doomed to partake in British ideas of sartorial elegance in order to profit British economic interests (Figure 3.11).[49] The accompanying text declares that "the popular advocates of civilization certainly are not the most civilized of individuals" before moving on to ask "what *is* civilisation?" and "have we such a superabundance of that commodity among us, that we should think about exporting it?"[50]

With Britain's close and continual encounters with far-away nations and peoples during a time of global expansion, *Punch* provided readers with a sense of

[Head of a Botecudo previous to disfigurement.]

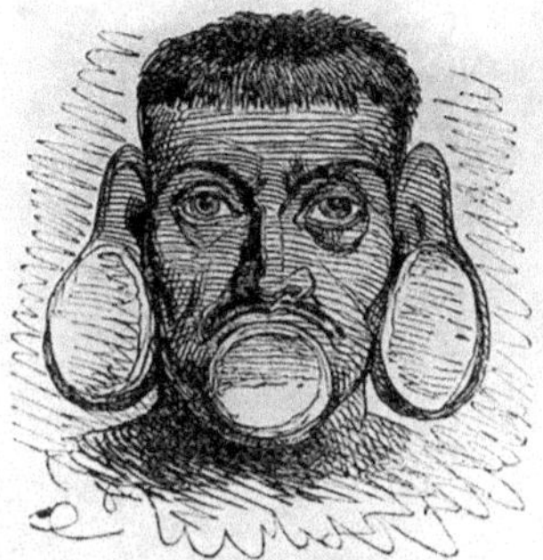

[Head of a Botecudo disfigured by chin and ear pendants.]

[Head of a Botecudo disfigured by civilization.]

FIGURE 3.11 "Untitled" *Punch*, Vol. 1 (1841), p. 27.

Source: Punch, or The London Charivari

FIGURE 3.12 "Back Again!" *Punch*, Vol. 85 (27 October 1883), p. 195.

Source: Punch, or The London Charivari

familiarity. The jabs at the disorderly lower classes or superficiality of the middle classes offered comic pleasure at a tumultuous time of rapid changes. Anxieties could be dispelled by laughing away social foibles, especially if the targets were obviously, and entertainingly, out of place and who better than the foreigner with differences in physiognomy and mannerisms? Codes of behaviour as well as social and racial hierarchies were lampooned and emphasised within the pages of *Punch*, and if unsettled, satirical attacks would swiftly fall upon the defector.

Foreign imitation of "Britishness" was held in contempt. The return to London by the Zulu king Cetewayo in 1883 prompted Sambourne to create "Back Again!" (Figure 3.12) in which Cetewayo wears a hybrid mix of African and English clothing. Gilbert à Beckett wrote accompanying verses

FIGURE 3.13 "Putting *His* Foot In It" *Punch*, Vol. 93 (10 December 1887), p. 267.

Source: Punch, or The London Charivari

stating that the *real* reason for the king's downfall by British military forces in 1879 and his inability to reign was due to being " 'spise" by his own people for becoming a "Masher" and dressing in "togs *à la mode*."[51] In another cartoon, George Du Maurier, the social etiquette aficionado, depicts a Japanese man in Western eveningwear, standing awkwardly as he talks with a seated woman who asks if "ladies' feet" in Japan are "still squeeze[d] up" (Figure 3.13). He explains how footbinding is a Chinese custom and thereby Japanese women could grow their feet "to quite their full size." He then blunders into an unintentional backhanded compliment by telling her, "Not that any would ever rival *yours*, Madam!"[52] Mannerism and dress were important and visually identifiable racial markers. Cetewayo and the Japanese, who were emergent imperial players, were disrupting established racial categories that were easily identifiable through sartorial distinction. Tastes and behavioural norms were what distinguished the British from "others" and for *Punch*, foreigners "may be able to put on Western clothing and learn British etiquette, but they could never be mistaken as British."[53]

The success of *Punch*'s Large Cuts lays in the fact that the men behind the magazine were adept at pinpointing the hottest topics of the day and the artists were skilled at creating clean, comical, and attractive images. The men were also conscious of the importance in tapping into readers' political awareness and thus the message in the Large Cuts was designed to be quickly understood. These visuals provide a glimpse into topics that were of utmost concern at particular moments in time. Many issues would undoubtedly have been unmentioned; as with any periodical press, *Punch* tailored its content to the interest of its readers in order to ensure its continued success.[54] At times, topics were selected for no other reason than the event was so talked about that it was simply unavoidable and there was certainly disagreements at the Table. Sambourne, for example, started as a junior artist and was conscious of the hierarchy at *Punch*. For the most part, the subjects of his cartoons were decided for him and thus the Large Cuts should be seen as a collective effort with the artist, at times, being dictated on what to draw. Although there were differences of opinion, a cartoon always emerged from the cacophony of debate and in generating the weekly Cuts, *Punch* not only engaged with issues at the forefront of public consciousness, but the magazine also played an important part in the shaping and dissemination of cultural and political knowledge.

Notes

1 Sambourne, 22 June 1897, Edward Linley Sambourne Diary.
2 Diane Peters, "A Celebration of Empire: Queen Victoria's Diamond Jubilee" *CAML Review/Revue de L'ACBM*, Vol. 26, No. 2 (1998), pp. 25–26.
3 Spielmann, *The History of "Punch,"* pp. 214–215.
4 Sambourne, 20, 21, 22 January 1901, 2 February 1901, Edward Linley Sambourne Diary.
5 Spielmann, *The History of "Punch,"* p. 215.
6 Spielmann, *The History of "Punch,"* p. 120.
7 Spielmann, *The History of "Punch,"* p. 110.
8 Frankie Morris, *Artist of Wonderland* (Cambridge: The Lutterworth Press, 2005), p. 225.

9 *Punch* ran from 1841–1992 then re-launched in 1996 until it closed permanently in 2002. "About" Punch Magazine Cartoon Archive. Online: https://www.punch.co.uk/about/index.
10 Leary, *The Punch Brotherhood*, p. 1. Leary states that the magazine was "not merely the most successful Victorian comic periodical, but – measured by circulation, influence, and longevity – one of the most successful magazines that has ever existed," p. 2.
11 Altick, *Punch*, p. 9.
12 Mayhew, *A Jorum of "Punch,"* p. VI.
13 Silver, 28 June 1860, Henry Silver Diary.
14 "Covent-Garden" *The Times*, 27 December 1842, p. 5.
15 Altick, *Punch*, pp. 11–12.
16 The *Westminster Review*, Vol. 38 (1842), July–October, pp. 316–317.
17 The *Westminster Review*, Vol. 38 (1842), July–October, p. 317.
18 James, *Partial Portraits*, pp. 334–335.
19 Spielmann, *The History of "Punch,"* pp. 5–6.
20 "The Moral of Punch" *Punch*, Vol. 1 (1841), p. 1.
21 John Ruskin, *The Art of England* (New York: John Wiley & Sons, 1884), p. 123.
22 Silver, 29 June 1864, Henry Silver Diary.
23 "The Moral of Punch" *Punch*, Vol. 1 (1841), p. 1.
24 Banta, *Barbaric Intercourse*, p. 25.
25 Spielmann, *The History of "Punch,"* pp. 187–188; see also Leary, *The Punch Brotherhood*, p. 35.
26 Brian Maidment, "Pencillings, Cuts and Cartoons: *Punch* and Early Victorian Comic Illustration" *Punch Historical Archive 1841–1992*. Cengage Learning, 2014. Online, n.p.
27 Altick, *Punch*, p. 124.
28 Leary, *The Punch Brotherhood*, p. 35.
29 Banta, *Barbaric Intercourse*, p. 19.
30 Spielmann, *The History of "Punch,"* pp. 168–169; Leary's *The Punch Brotherhood* discusses in great detail the Table talks of the *Punch* members of staff.
31 Spielmann, *The History of 'Punch,'* p. 146.
32 The service at St. Paul's never transpired due to receipt of a cable from the American minister at Beijing, whose message conflicted with the newspaper's articles. James Hevia, *English Lessons: The Pedagogy of Imperialism in Nineteenth-century China* (Durham: Hong Kong: Duke University Press, 2003), p. 192.
33 Leary, *The Punch Brotherhood*, p. 42.
34 Silver, 1 July 1863, Henry Silver Diary.
35 Leary, *The Punch Brotherhood*, p. 47.
36 Layard, *Shirley Brooks of "Punch,"* pp. 115–116.
37 Layard, *Shirley Brooks of "Punch,"* p. 165.
38 Leary, *The Punch Brotherhood*, p. 47.
39 Leary, *The Punch Brotherhood*, p. 52.
40 Silver, 10 May 1865, Henry Silver Diary; cited in Leary, *The Punch Brotherhood*, p. 52.
41 Silver, 7 November 1864, Henry Silver Diary.
42 *Daily Telegraph* (27 February 1914) as cited in Morris, *Artist of Wonderland*, p. 225.
43 Charles L. Graves, *Mr. Punch's History of Modern England*, Vol. II (London: Cassell and Company, Ltd., 1921), p. 25.
44 Silver, 27 May 1868, Henry Silver Diary.
45 "The Revolt League Against Eyre" *Punch*, Vol. 54 (30 May 1868), p. 237.
46 Millar, "The Life of 'Punch'," p. 877.
47 Michael Cohen, "Imagining Militarism: Art Young and *The Masses* Face the Enemy" *Radical History Review*, No. 106 (Winter 2010), p. 97; Richard Scully, "Constructing the

Colossus: The Origins of Linley Sambourne's Greatest 'Punch' Cartoon" *International Journal of Comic Art*, Vol. 14, No. 2 (2012), p. 136.
48 "Eastward Ho!" *Punch*, Vol. 107 (11 August 1894), p. 63.
49 Banta, *Barbaric Intercourse*, p. 33.
50 "Civilisation" *Punch*, Vol. 1 (1841), p. 27.
51 "Back Again!" *Punch*, Vol. 85 (27 October 1883), p. 195.
52 "Putting *His* Foot in It" *Punch*, Vol. 93 (10 December 1887), p. 267.
53 Amy Matthewson, "Satirising Imperial Anxiety in Victorian Britain: Representing Japan in *Punch* Magazine, 1852–1893" *Contemporary Japan* (2021), p. 19.
54 Altick, *Punch*, p. XXI.

4

"A CHINESE PUZZLE"[1]

The trajectory of negating China

Two months after the opening of the Great Exhibition of 1851, John Tenniel created "The Happy Family in Hyde Park" (Figure 4.1) and represented the event as harmonious internationalism bringing the people of the world together. Percival Leigh wrote the accompanying text, highlighting how the "British Lion" is "on the best of terms both with his-self and everybody helse" and is the "monarch of all he surveys." It moves on to highlight the amity of nations; the "Bear of Roosha" was noted for his "remarkable gentleness of disposition" and "wonderful improvement of his temper" made by changing his diet to "plum-pudding." The ferocious Bengal Tiger now enjoys a game of leapfrog and the "Great Indian Elephant is amusin' his-self by feedin' the Chinese Pig with gingerbread nuts."[2] Tenniel's corresponding Large Cut visualises the textual description of the world joyfully participating in the event. Prince Albert, the royal patron of the Exhibition, stands outside the Crystal Palace bringing attention to the global community all merrily dancing within the glass walls. Upon closer inspection, however, the image reveals a more discordant state of affairs.

Prince Albert stands with other European figures, directing their attention to the exotic foreigners put on display. Jeffrey A. Auerbach explains how the "alien others" are "separated behind the glass windows of the Crystal Palace" as if they are specimens in "a museum case of a circus cage, engaged in a bizarre and perhaps primitive dance."[3] With such a mixture of class and race, the Crystal Palace became a voyeuristic spectacle, a place to see and be seen, and the exhibits themselves became of secondary importance. Europe, imagined as a united entity, formed part of the only group thought capable of agency and therefore take their place as viewers, albeit from a careful distance, gazing upon the uncivilised.[4] The odd combination of races was made more peculiar with the addition of different social classes within British society coming together. *Punch* ridiculed the working classes

DOI: 10.4324/9781003025573-4

THE HAPPY FAMILY IN HYDE PARK.

FIGURE 4.1 "The Happy Family in Hyde Park" *Punch*, Vol. 21 (19 July 1851), p. 38.

Source: Punch, or The London Charivari

rubbing shoulders with "their betters" while simultaneously using foreignness as a convenient visual "other" to bring Britons of all classes together.

This chapter traces the trajectory of *Punch*'s changing perspective of China from the 1840s to the 1860s. The first three decades brought about a change in tone and outlook, beginning with playful condescension before slipping into scornful condemnation. Throughout the 1840s, *Punch*'s engagement with China focused either on concerns over tea, a foreign commodity that was becoming an essential product in British daily life, or on civilising missions, in which the target for criticism was on the British, not the Chinese. There were, however, commentaries reflecting a sense of superiority in Britain's recent victory in the First Opium War and China was positioned as technologically backward in comparison to Britain. By 1851, the magazine re-directed its attention to the Great Exhibition with its reportage incorporating comic jabs at the British social class system as well as textual and visual quips at foreigners in London attending the event.

By examining *Punch*'s commentaries on peoples and events surrounding the Great Exhibition, the magazine reveals dynamics of power imbalances in the British social class system as well as wider anxieties of Britain's own position within the international community. Caricatures of the Chinese were employed as a convenient visual contrast to notions of "Britishness" and the cartoons utilised race as a tool of differentiation to produce a unified British identity. No matter how different the working classes were to the upper classes, they were still British subjects and could claim, whether imagined or not, a shared system of values, mannerisms, and tastes. By the end of the 1850s, Britain and China were once again engaged in open hostilities in the Arrow War, also known as the Second Opium War. This time, the sense of playful patriotism that permeated commentaries of the First Opium War was replaced by vitriolic contempt for China and the Chinese, reflecting developments in Sino-British relations as well as the general negation of China in the British popular imagination.

China defeated

Playful condescension

Nathan Dunn's Chinese Collection opened in London on 23 June 1842 and was met with much enthusiasm. Dunn, an American merchant and philanthropist, spent twelve years as a trader in China and was allowed to amass such a collection in gratitude by the Canton authorities for refusing to deal in opium.[5] The collection was first opened in Philadelphia in 1831 before making its way to London where it was housed in a pagoda in Hyde Park Corner that was purposely built for the exhibit.[6] It displayed 1,341 items and was "the largest and most comprehensive assemblage of Chinese artefacts of the day."[7] The exhibition came complete with gilt idols and scowling dragons, replicas of Chinese streets and shops as well as the interior of a private Chinese home.[8] Madame Tussaud contributed wax figurines of Commissioner Lin and his Favourite Concubine[9] as well as a Chinese couple positioned to look like spectators, with the wife moving her head as she spoke to her husband.[10]

The collection arrived when Britain recently emerged victorious in the First Opium War and there was curiosity for information on the defeated nation. The accompanying London edition of the catalogue sold more than 300,000 copies and the exhibition itself was maintained for several years before returning to America.[11]

The purpose was to educate through the visual, "by *things* rather than words,"[12] and thus the collection provided an instructional display into perceived national characteristics of the peoples of China. The *Illustrated London News* commented that the exhibit:

> Analyse the mental and moral qualities of the Chinese, and gather some knowledge of their idols, their temples, their pagodas, their bridges, their arts, their sciences, their manufactures, their fancies, their parlours, their drawing rooms. . . . Here we have, not one object, but thousands; not a single discovery, but an empire with all its variety of light and shade, its experience, [and] its mind.[13]

Dunn's exhibition became a space where the collected material culture was promoted as knowledge not just about China, but represented a true reflection of the mindset of the people.

Due to the popularity of the exhibition, *Punch* not only reported on the collection in their weekly journal, but a satirical guidebook was also published, titled *Punch's Guide to the Chinese Exhibition at Knightsbridge*. The focus in the periodical and the guidebook was on providing mocking commentaries on the ineptitude of the Chinese army, the despotic nature of the Emperor, and the dilapidated conditions of antiquated Chinese military technology. The interest on Chinese armoury, considered "the most attractive portion of the exhibition," was due to the fact that "[Britons] are at war" with China. However, the weapons on display were ridiculed, dismissing notions that China was, in any way, a threat to Britain. Chinese bows and arrows were pronounced "their best weapons, for if they hurt nobody else with them, at least they don't hurt themselves." The shields were described as "the most truly destructive of all their instruments of war" because the Chinese "paint such dreadful faces, that the very sight of them has been known to make English soldiers fall down, and almost die – of laughing." Even the Duke of Wellington could not contain his amusement when confronted with the glass cases filled with Chinese weaponry. It was reported that he simply "turned his head away and smiled."[14]

Chinese weapons were not the only satirical targets; the Chinese military was mocked for its inefficiency and lack of courage. *Punch's Guide to the Chinese Exhibition at Knightsbridge* is replete with quips regarding the Chinese army "running away" as the "grand military manoeuvre . . . which is the most perfect feat of the Chinese soldiery."[15] In one cartoon, the Chinese military is in disarray during its flight from the battlefield; by contrast, the calm and orderly British army is seen approaching in the background, ready for battle (Figure 4.2). The notion of a tyrannical Chinese Emperor is used as explanation for such cowardly military behaviour. *Punch* explains that the "most anxious parent never whipped his children more frequently" and this supposed liberal use of corporal punishment is juxtaposed with the British. Chinese whippings "seems to be the very antipodes of English, for there they often whip people's *heads* off."[16]

FIGURE 4.2 "Chinese Soldiers retiring from Service" *Punch's Guide to the Chinese Exhibition at Knightsbridge*, Vol. 21 (1851), p. 39.

Source: Punch, or The London Charivari

The placement of China in binary opposition to Britain provided readers with a shared sense of value and principles. The description of Chinese soldiers as cowards led by a cruel tyrant constructed and reinforced perceived notions and ideas of "oriental manners" and this created a sense of "Britishness" in underscoring a familiarity in the way "we" behave that is entirely unlike "them." While seemingly playful in nature, *Punch* produced a set of principles such as honour, rational, and righteousness, and set them against the imagined follies and disgraceful behaviour of "others."[17] *Punch*'s ridiculing of Chinese armoury, on one level, dispelled any anxieties over the war with China; the commentaries suggested that China's antiquated military was no match against Britain's technologically advanced equipment. There were, however, deeper implications.

Already in the eighteenth century, European ideas of productivity and progress along with the speed of development during the Industrial Revolution reinforced notions of superiority.[18] *Punch*'s remarks coincided with broader narratives of China as a symbolic stagnant country, an idea that came to dominate the discourse on China in the British imagination by the mid-nineteenth century. The jibes may have been created with the intention to produce a sense of fun, but underneath the layer of joviality lies a sense of superiority imbedded in notions of progress. The arrival of a Chinese junk named *Keying* in March 1848 prompted more material for comparison. The vessel was nothing the British public had ever seen before, yet it was an example of Chinese shipbuilding – a technology that the British were well acquainted with. *Keying* was described in *Punch* as "a real ship, mounted with real guns, and a sail made like an immense door-mat" and concluded that "everything is curious about it" and that it "is the most perfect Chinese puzzle we ever saw."[19] *Keying* served as both an exotic object of curiosity as well as something familiar and it caused quite a lot of excitement when it docked on the Thames.

The British press not only reported on the "oddity" of the vessel itself, but also reports were made when the crew aboard *Keying* decided to stage a series of performances. Crew members announced a "gigantic Balloon Residence" titled "The Flying Palace of Aladdin" as well as a "dance on the deck, surrounded by Lanterns, Flying Fish, Fiery Dragons, etc." The dance, which promised to be in the native manner, was accompanied by singing, which was compared to the "impromptu feline discourse, which we sometimes hear on housetops at dead of night."[20] The French composer Hector Berlioz described the singing as "wildcat howls" and "turkey cluckings" and ended by stating that he "shall with difficulty be persuaded that the Chinese are not demented."[21] Residents in the area appeared to have been in agreement and the City Navigation Committee issued an order for the music to cease. Nothing more was reported on *Keying* after that point and in 1853, she was towed to River Mersey and abandoned.[22]

Amidst the quips about China's "puzzling" military technology and the principles held by Chinese soldiers, *Punch* was deeply concerned over trade and Britain's dependence on the foreign commodity of tea. Commenting on the British victory in the First Opium War and the indemnity imposed on China, an article titled "The Peace with China" remarked,

> tea will be dearer now than it has ever been before; for it happens that the Chinese have undertaken to pay 21 millions of dollars without having a single rap towards it; and they intend to raise the money by taxing every pound of tea that is exported from the country. Thus, what we receive with one hand we shall pay with the other.[23]

Britain may have won the battle but in reality, it was China who won the war. By heavily taxing tea, a commodity that Britons could not do without, the flow of silver would be in China's favour and to illustrate the point further, a songsheet, "The Queen's Speech – Peace with China" sarcastically celebrates Britain's victory by allowing China to "tax our tea" in order to pay the indemnity.[24]

The history of tea-drinking in Britain dates back to the seventeenth and eighteenth centuries when tea was a luxury product and a symbol of wealth and status since only the aristocracy was able to afford its consumption. In the last decades of the eighteenth century, imports of tea rose from less than one million to over ten million pounds (in weight).[25] By the nineteenth century, it had become a necessity. In *Tea, Its Mystery and History*, Samuel Phillips Day explains that tea was "the only real luxury which is common to rich and poor alike"[26] and by the 1840s, tea, along with white bread, were the staple diet of even the poorest labourers. Day quotes an unnamed "eminent statesman" who asserts,

> What was first regarded as a luxury, has now become, if not an absolute necessity, at least one of our accustomed daily wants, the loss of which would cause more suffering and excite more regret than would the deprivation of many things which once were counted as necessaries of life.[27]

Between 1841 and 1850, the average consumption of tea, per annum, per head was 1.6 lb; this increased to 2.31 lbs in the following decade and by 1891–1900, the average Briton was consuming 5.7 lb. of tea per year. Table 4.1 demonstrates the striking rise of tea consumption in the United Kingdom, including Ireland.[28]

TABLE 4.1 Table of Tea Consumption[29]

Period	*Average number of lb. of tea consumed per annum*	*Average consumption per head per annum in lb.*
1851–1860	65,160,456	2.31
1861–1870	97,775,548	3.26
1871–1880	144,462,622	4.37
1881–1890	178,130,836	4.92
1891–1900	224,176,800	5.70

By the nineteenth century, tea had become the nation's habitual beverage but its symbol of British identity rested on a foreign product imported from China. Sino-British relations therefore became fraught due to Britain's dependency on Chinese tea that tipped the balance of trade in China's favour.

A possible solution suggested by *Punch* was to "bully the Celestials into adopting our wants and habits as their own which- as the usual cry about civilisation has been already got up – will no doubt be the consequence." The article continues,

> We shall, perhaps, teach them that bald heads and barbarism are synonymous – a conviction which, if once knocked into them, will give an impetus to our wig-manufacturers; and if, under the pretext of civilisation, we can compel them to put on bear-skin coats, with souweater hats, we shall impart a refreshing buoyancy to the slop-market.
>
> . . .
>
> Now that the Chinese are doomed to "civilisation," they may make up their minds to be bullied, robbed, and swindled in every direction; for, in the political vocabulary, "to civilise the people of a distant country," has a meaning which the treatment of the Indians in North America will give a pretty accurate solution of.[30]

Punch recognised the uselessness of wigs, "bear-skin coats," and "souweater hats" to the Chinese market and highlighted commercial subjugation concealed in the narrative of "civilisation" which "the Chinese are doomed to."[31]

In "Peace with the Pig-Tails," Douglas Jerrold, writing under the initial "Q," criticised politicians and merchants who, "in the anticipative eye of profit, already see the Emperor of China clothed in a Manchester shirt, all his wives in Manchester cotton, and the whole of his court handling Sheffield knives and forks."[32] Jerrold, always critical of establishments and social hierarchies, was particularly scornful of profiteering couched under the rubric of "civilising missions." He railed against the divergence of funds to missions abroad when resources were badly needed for philanthropic efforts within British society.[33] Eight years later, his scorn did not abate. In 1850, Jerrold questioned the morality of Britain's global trade practices in attempting to fulfil the "Manchester dream" which is the "vision that shows that every Chinaman in a night-cap of cotton is to be realised by the percussion caps of English infantry."[34]

Punch's attitude towards China in the early 1840s was a combination of playfulness mixed with a sense of superiority. The real target of attacks was British social and political ills and Jerrold's distinctive venomous style of expressing his disapproval was felt within the general tone of the magazine. *Punch*'s initial radicalism in its early years tended to use China and the Chinese simply as a tool to make pointed social and political criticisms on British issues. A good example is found in "Exhibition of the English in China," in which a satirical exhibition by a Chinese "Dunn from Pekin" who "has sojourned many years in England." The collection features "the faces and fashions of the barbarian English" with an accompanying "catalogue of our good and bad qualities." Displays include an exhausted and overworked needlewoman crying onto her work (Figure 4.3) and

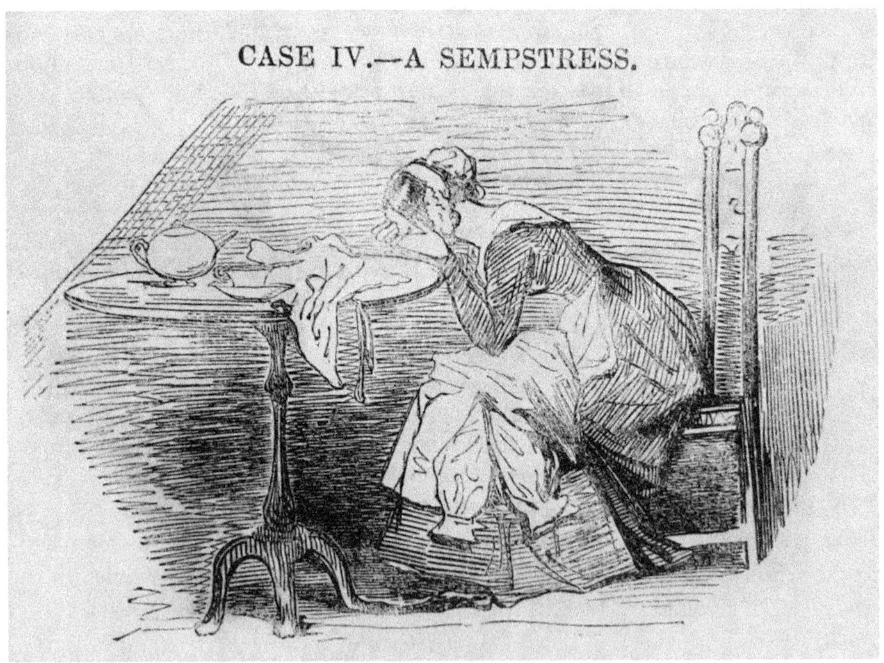

FIGURE 4.3 "Case IV. – A Sempstress" *Punch*, Vol. 6 (1844), p. 220.

Source: Punch, or The London Charivari

FIGURE 4.4 "Case IX. – A Shopkeeper" *Punch*, Vol. 6 (1844), p. 221.

Source: Punch, or The London Charivari

a greedy and cunning shopkeeper, represented as a fox rubbing his hands together (Figure 4.4).[35]

The employment of a "foreign observer" has been a popular and traditional tool used by satirists to explore national values and principles. In the eighteenth century, Montesquieu's *Persian Letters* and Oliver Goldsmith's *The Citizen of the World* used fictitious Oriental observers to challenge claims of universal truths and highlight a nation's political and social foibles. While it is the satirist's own nation that is the obvious subject of attack, the ideological use of "Orientals" maintained stereotypes and underscored difference through racial physiognomy as well as supposed manners and customs.[36]

Punch used China as an "Oriental observer," an already familiar satirical tool, to lampoon a variety of domestic issues and raise disconcerting questions about the state of British society. Who, *Punch* asks its readers, are the real barbarians and what ethical values equate to a nation that can claim to be civilised? Throughout the 1840s, the magazine's comments on the First Opium War, British dependency on tea as well as foreign trade, reveal an awareness of a global community. By 1851, this consciousness moved away from its radical stance and *Punch* re-directed its focus towards events surrounding the Great Exhibition when China, along with "foreign others," were employed, not as a vehicle to ask unsettling questions or critic a variety of social ills, but to solidify a sense of British identity.

The great exhibition

The familiar and the foreign

On May Day 1851, Queen Victoria opened the first international exhibition at the Crystal Palace in Hyde Park. Aptly named the Great Exhibition, it was a tremendous success with over 15,000 contributors whose objects were displayed along more than ten miles and were viewed by over six million visitors, almost a fifth of the entire British population.[37] The purpose of the event was twofold: firstly, it was an instructional display about the processes of industrialisation during a period of heightened tensions among discontented industrial workers and participants of the Chartist movement. Secondly, it was a display of imperialism and power represented by manufactured goods and industrial wealth from nations around the world. The event was officially organised by Prince Albert and its policy was to include and encourage the attendance of the working class. Organisers' recognised that the Exhibition was made possible by the results produced by this sector of society.

There was also an educational component to the event. It was believed that through guidance and education, the working class would achieve a strong sense of national identity that would trump ideas of class revolt or revolution that was happening in parts across Europe.[38] The industrial economy gave rise to rapid urban population growth and masses of people residing in new industrial cities were viewed with suspicion by the upper and middle classes due to the possibilities for revolutionary activities. The new industry workers were also becoming conscious of their economic hardships and aware of their political potential.[39] Frederick William of Prussia wrote to Prince Albert, the official organiser of the Great Exhibition, expressing his fears that there will be a mass disruption in London during the event. Prince Albert replied, "In England . . . we fear neither risings nor murderous attacks."[40] However, this expression of confidence in the British public faltered when, a few days later, organisers tried to ban the public from attending the May Day Opening Ceremony in order to protect Queen Victoria (a decision later overturned).[41]

Feelings of fear and snobbery had organisers apprehensive of potential "mobs" of working class Britons mingling with the middle and upper classes. One solution was to offer varying admission prices on different days. Season tickets could be purchased at £3 3s "for a gentleman" and £2 2s "for a lady" and only those with season tickets were permitted on the opening day. On the second and third day, the fee was reduced to £1; on the fourth, it dropped to 5s until 26 May when the fee would be 1s from Monday to Thursday, 2s 6d on Fridays, and 5s on Saturdays and organisers agreed that children under the age of 13 would be admitted at half price.[42] The division of entrance prices allowed people of the middle and upper classes to choose whether or not they preferred to segregate themselves. Lord Palmerston, for example, chose to attend only on Saturdays when the admission fee was set at the highest price and would therefore reduce the ability of the working classes to attend.[43]

When the Great Exhibition finally opened, the working classes showed interest and many made their way to London. Those coming from the industrial northern part of the country came in great numbers with estimates between 750,000 and 1,000,000.[44] The event became one of the rare and few occasions during the Victorian era that allowed social classes from across Britain to come in close proximity of each other. Although there were no revolts, the codes of conduct between the classes varied substantially and different classes occupied different spaces within the Crystal Palace, with the respectable classes generally gathering around the British Nave where John Bell's Shakespeare Statue was displayed. This changed during the last week of the Exhibition when the working classes congregated in that area to eat their packed lunches and nurse their children.[45]

John Leech's "Dinner-Time at the Crystal Palace" captures the working class standing and sitting around the Shakespeare Statue (Figure 4.5). One woman with a picnic lunch speaks to another who sits with breast exposed as she nurses her baby. A man stands to the side as he pours some kind of spirit into a glass while the woman next to him slumps against a plinth, either from too much drink or from sheer exhaustion. Leech added "One touch of nature makes the whole world kin" on the plinth, suggesting togetherness; there is no divide between Shakespeare and the working class. In "The Pound and the Shilling" (Figure 4.6), the Duke of Wellington, flanked by two fashionable ladies, meet the working class. The navvy and carpenter, distinguished by their attire, appear confident and do not step aside or divert their gazes when in front of their "betters." The outward appearance of congenial class integration is deceiving.

Jeffrey Auerback explains how the caption for this image can be read two ways:

> "Whoever thought of meeting *you* here," suggesting that the social classes in Victorian England were generally segregated and that respectable society had assumed the Crystal Palace to be part of their domain; or, "Whoever thought of meeting you *here*," meaning that there were places where the classes mingled, but that respectable society did not consider the Crystal Palace to be one of them.[46]

Leech's Large Cuts manage to simultaneously promote and challenge the Great Exhibition's declaration of harmony between the classes. There was indeed cohesion, however, tensions persisted. John Tallis, author of *History and Description of the Crystal Palace*, claimed that "all social distinctions were for the moment merged in the general feeling of pride and admiration at the wondrous result of science and labour" and that "Never before in England had there been so free and general a mixture of classes as

DINNER-TIME AT THE CRYSTAL PALACE.

FIGURE 4.5 "Dinner-time at the crystal palace" *punch*, vol. 21 (5 July 1851), p. 16.
Source: Punch, or The London Charivari

under that roof."[47] The geologist and palaeontologist Gideon Mantell, however, felt differently. He recorded in his diary that in the nave, he observed "many dirty women with their infants, giving suck on the seats with their breasts uncovered" and that there were many "vulgar, ignorant, country people" at the Crystal Palace. He grumbled at the "truly absurd" idea that the "splendid, marvellous, incredible exhibition of nature and art" could possibly be "appreciated by the ignorant mobs."[48]

FIGURE 4.6 "The Pound and the Shilling" *Punch*, Vol. 20 (14 June 1851), p. 247.

Source: Punch, or The London Charivari

It is difficult to discern who is the target of ridicule in Leech's "Dinner-Time at the Crystal Palace" and "The Pound and the Shilling." Are these images criticising the snobbery of the middle classes or simply trying to dispel anxieties of social mixing between the classes? In reality, it is debatable whether the Exhibition was a success or failure in bringing together Britain as a nation, regardless of class or regional differences. Some hailed the event as a symbol of progress and technological achievement that signified class harmony. Others claimed that the event was for the benefit of the middle and upper classes and most of the working class chose not to attend while those living in impoverished conditions could not.[49] When you take into consideration the varying admission prices allowing those who wish to separate themselves from the working class to visit on different days, visitor guides instructing the working class how to behave,[50] as well as snide remarks such as those recorded by Mantell, class integration was clearly viewed with both suspicion and apprehension.

The Great Exhibition was, however, consistent in its sense of nationalism and a central theme that ran through the entire Exhibition was one of systematic classification. As an event with a strong educational component, knowledge about different "types" of nations and their goods were highlighted in order to provide Victorians with a particular narrative about Britain's relations with its empire and colonies. The Indian court was of extreme interest, and the display both supported and legitimatised Britain's possession of a disempowered nation. The object most representative of British rule was the empty Indian royal throne that was placed at the centre of the exhibition space. The seat of Indian power was, quite literally, empty and thereby created an impression that it was up for the taking; this would symbolically come to pass when Queen Victoria was declared Empress of India in 1877.[51] The Indian exhibit also shaped Victorian notions about the benefits of colonial possession in providing raw materials. The display of the Koh-i-Noor, the largest diamond in the world, was a sensation. *The Crystal Palace* emphasised the "higher interest to the future destinies of our vast Indian empire" through the development of railways and roads under British rule that would allow manufacturers access to "cotton, sugar, rice, linseed, hemp, and other staples."[52]

The Great Exhibition not only displayed technological achievements and manufactured goods, but visitors to the Crystal Palace were also, in a sense, put on display. *The Times* reported, "the people have now become the exhibition"[53] and a central recurring theme was the "un-Britishness" of foreigners who came to London. Some rejoiced in the potential to build international understanding and cooperation. Richard Cobden, for example, hoped the Exhibition would usher in an era of international peace and "break down barriers that have separated the people of different nations, and witness the universal republic."[54] Others, however, held foreigners with contempt and suspicion. Addressing the House of Commons on 26 July 1850, Colonel Charles de Laet Waldo Sibthorp, the Tory M.P. from Lincoln, expressed xenophobic sentiments as the reason to reject hosting the event

> ,An exhibition of the industry of all nations, forsooth! An exhibition of the trumpery and trash of foreign countries. . . . They are flying in the face of the rights of the public merely to gratify the foreigner, *who had no right to be here at all.*[55]

A number of Britons were so concerned about the arrival of foreigners, they wrote to the Duke of Wellington with suggestions such as keeping the navy on continual patrol (especially around the coast of Ireland), cordoning off London, or increasing police presence fourfolds.[56]

In "The Year of Expectations," Horace Mayhew, was contemptuous of xenophobic sentiments. He wrote,

> Every bigotted Englishman, belonging to the fine old JOHN BULL school . . . expects to see every foreigner with long moustachios, long beard, and long hair, and dirty habits . . . and expects that London will be troubled with nothing less than the Plague in consequence.[57]

Mayhew's opinion was not, however, always in agreement with his colleagues at *Punch*; John Leech, for example, held very different views. It was well known that Leech disliked foreigners and while Mayhew ridiculed British fear of foreigners, Leech provided a different perspective. In his "The Great Derby Race of 1851," all the nations of the world compete in the race for industrial advancement in front of the Great Exhibition (Figure 4.7).

In the lead, and the clear winner, is Britain, represented by John Bull riding a bull, Joseph Paxton, the man who designed the Crystal Palace, running along quick as lightning, and Mr. Punch, riding his dog Toby. Lagging behind

FIGURE 4.7 "The Great Derby Race for Eighteen Hundred and Fifty-One" *Punch*, Vol. 20 (24 May 1851), pp. 213–215.

Source: Punch, or The London Charivari

is the rest of the world, riding with determination on an assortment of animals from giraffes, elephants, ostriches, and camels. Set apart from the other nations is China, represented by a fat Chinese man with his eyes closed to industrial progress astride a pig who is facing the wrong direction. The crowd observing this bizarre race is the English, standing united together on the sidelines. A man in the crowd points to China while another throws his head back in laughter. When it comes to technological advancement, it appears that China is nothing more than a laughing stock.

China was the only nation that declined to participate and did not contribute to the Great Exhibition. The China exhibit was therefore cobbled together by organisers who relied on contributions from merchants trading in Canton as well as private collectors. The result was an odd assortment of objects and the general consensus was that the China display was the most disappointing of all the nations.[58] The refusal to take part in the event must have surprised the organisers and brought back memories from previous non-cooperation when the Qianlong Emperor rejected all British requests in the failed 1793 Macartney mission.[59] The Great Exhibition was intended to symbolise Western education and technological advancements; it was also representative of free trade, an economic principle believed to be an essential element for political liberty and international peace.[60] China's apparent disregard for these concepts was shocking; John R. Davis points out, "this rejection seemed tantamount to a denial of a universal truth, and therefore both loathsome and absurd – and the Chinese . . . became the antiheroes of the Exhibition."[61]

Leech's 1853 centrefold, titled "The Great Barbarian Dragon That Will Eat Up 'The Brother of the Moon,' &c. &c. &c." (Figure 4.8) represents China ready to battle Western notions of modernity and progress. In the background are familiar symbols of "Chineseness" in the British imagination such as a pagoda, bridge with three figures holding lanterns, and a willow tree. In the foreground, a rotund Chinese Emperor with his army of soldiers stand ready to fight against technological advancement, represented by the train with the word "progress" clearly written on the side. In the space between the front of the train and the Chinese army, a Chinese man attempts to retreat from a pair of scissors poised to cut off his queue. The queue, a characteristic Manchu male hairstyle, was a strong visual marker of "Chineseness" and the artists at *Punch* frequently used this as an object of ridicule, whether playfully or otherwise. The hairstyle was also an instantly recognisable symbol that denotes difference.

Richard Doyle used the queue to represent China in "May Day, Eighteen Hundred and Fifty-One." Mr. Punch sits on a throne next to Lady Britannia, the British Lion by her side and Toby, Mr. Punch's faithful companion, next to him (Figure 4.9). They observe the world coming to praise Britain's industrial strength as depicted by men from a multitude of nations, holding up an arm in reverence. China is represented by two familiar symbols: tea and the queue. Unlike the other nations who are struggling with the size of their crates full of goods, China only has tea to offer. At the front, a Chinese man in "traditional" Mandarin dress complete

FIGURE 4.8 "The Great Barbarian Dragon That Will Eat Up 'The Brother of the Moon,' &c. &c. &c." *Punch*, Vol. 25 (3 September 1853), pp. 98–99.

Source: Punch, or The London Charivari

with clog-style shoes and a conical hat, holds a tea set upon a tray and is unable to move because of a dog pulling at his long queue. The queue was also used as part of decorative initials that was interspersed within the pages of *Punch*; for example, Gilbert à Beckett's initial for "Magnetic Ministry" depicts a Chinese man reading a newspaper, his queue flung over the letter "A" (Figure 4.10).

The history of the queue may not have been fully understood by most Britons but its importance was known. British sailors on the H.M.S. *Nemesis* knew the symbolic significance of the hairstyle when they cut them off of the Chinese that surrendered during the First Opium War, aware that it was a mark of deep disgrace. In 1858, the British again used the cutting of queues to humiliate who they deemed to be troublemakers in Canton.[62] *Punch*'s textual commentaries on the Chinese frequently played on the word "tail" for comedic effect; however, the play on words also resulted in giving this hairstyle "resonances of animality."[63] The queue was a distinguishing and familiar visual feature of what it meant to be Chinese and it served as a powerful symbol of difference, immediately separating the Chinese from the British. Differences in tastes were also highlighted. Figure 4.11 depicts a London dining room where a server repeats the order of a Chinese customer, "very nice Birds' Nest Soup, Sir! – Yes, Sir! Rat Pie, Sir, Just up. – Yes, Sir! – And a nice little Dog to foller – Yes, Sir!"[64] To the right, an English gentleman with his wife looks startled at the scene before them.

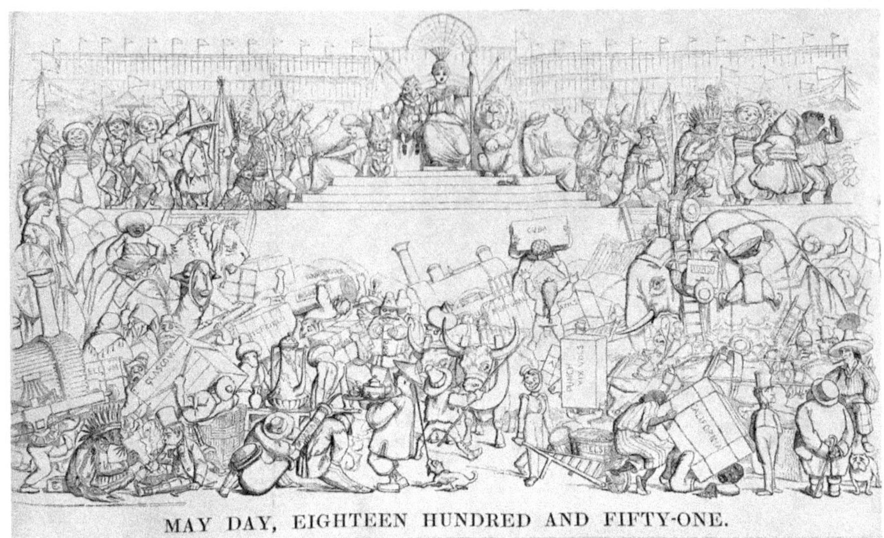

FIGURE 4.9 "May Day, Eighteen Hundred and Fifty-One" *Punch*, Vol. 20 (3 May 1851), pp. 179–181.

Source: Punch, or The London Charivari

Punch's representations of China and the Chinese during the Great Exhibition offer a different perspective when compared to the magazine's portrayal of the British working class. While both take a condescending tone, the Chinese were so very "Other" in their physiognomy, fashion, and tastes and became part of *Punch*'s repertoire of the foreign spectacle, in which the imagined reader would not relate nor be able to identify with. These "Chinese characteristic traits" were based on stereotypes, which the magazine happily reinforced and maintained, but what happens when these systems of classification are suddenly disrupted? The appearance of He-Sing, a Chinese man mistaken for a Mandarin at the opening ceremonies of the Crystal Palace on 30 April 1851 unsettled rigid class markers. Dressed in embroidered silk, nobody knew who He-Sing was but the sight of him greeting the Duke of Wellington led people to believe that he was a Chinese Mandarin.

During the singing of the Hallelujah chorus, He-Sing suddenly, and to everyone's amusement, jostled his way to the front of the throne and began bowing repeatedly to Queen Victoria. As his identity remained unknown, He-Sing formed part of the procession and was included in the official watercolour that commemorated the event.[65] It was not until the ceremonies were over that it became known that He-Sing was not a Mandarin at all but a resident on the Chinese junk *Keying* moored in the Thames and was only trying to drum up business by attending the Great Exhibition.[66] William Thackeray recorded the event by commenting, "There was a Chinese with a face like a pantomime mask . . . who went up and kissed the Duke of Wellington much to the old boy's surprise, and the Queen looked not uninteresting (sic)."[67]

FIGURE 4.10 "Untitled" *Punch*, Vol. 24 (18 June 1853), p. 249.

Source: Punch, or The London Charivari

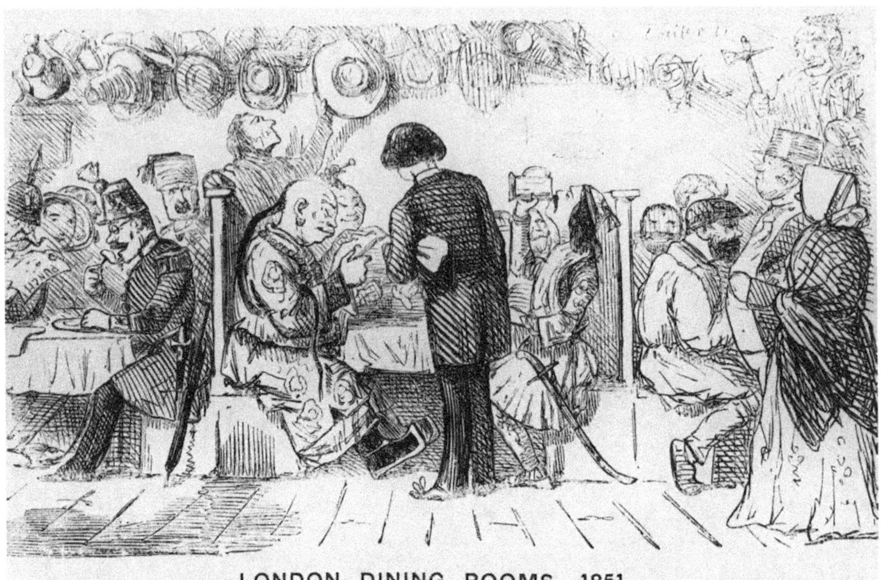

FIGURE 4.11 "London Dining Rooms, 1851" *Punch Almanack for 1851*, n.p.

Source: Punch, or The London Charivari

Gilbert à Beckett's summary of events took on a tone of indignation:

> At the conclusion of the ceremonial, a Chinese, carried away, or rather pushed forward, by his enthusiasm, performed suddenly, before HER MAJESTY, an elaborate salaam, consisting of a sudden act of prostration on his face, and when the individual rose up, the custom at once occurred to us as the cause of the general flatness of features and particular squareness of nose of that flowery people, who, from their countenance, appear to have been sown broad-cast over a large tract of country.[68]

The description of He-Sing performing "an elaborate salaam" pokes fun at what Europeans call the *kowtow*. Much like China's "non-cooperation" in refusing to participate in the Great Exhibition, the *kowtow* was a significant gesture that encapsulated contentions in Sino-British relations that dated back to Lord Macartney's embassy to the Qianlong court in 1793. For Britons, the *kowtow* stood in polar opposition to "the Victorian gentleman and maker of empire" who was always represented as "stalwartly upright, touching the ground with more than one knee only when wounded or dead at the hands of savage barbarians."[69] In 1851, the *kowtow*, seen as a quintessentially Chinese gesture, came to Britain, in the midst of London, and at the heart of an event celebrating progress and modernity.[70]

The arrival of a performing Chinese family around the corner from the Great Exhibition provided another unsettling occasion when class boundaries were blurred. The *Illustrated London News* described the family encompassing "a Chinese Lady, named Pwan-ye-Koo, with small lotus-feet only 2½ inches in length, a Chinese professor of music, his two children (a boy and a girl), the *femme de chamber* of the lady, and an interpreter" who are credited for presenting "an image in high relief of the native manners of a Chinese family."[71] Mayhew wrote in *Punch*:

> We confess the Chinese Lady, at the Chinese collection, is a Chinese Puzzle to us. We do not deny her Celestial beauty – nor do we deny the smallness of her foot. Her singing, also, is as perfect as Chinese singing can be; but we are puzzled as to the fact of her being "*a lady of quality*." We are told that she occupied a very fashionable position at Canton, where she was the *belle* for one of two seasons. This is a puzzle to us. We cannot understand how "a Lady of Quality" can lend herself to a shilling exhibition.[72]

The focus and primary concern was whether or not Pwan-ye-Koo was "*a lady of quality*," a reputation called into question due to her apparent willingness to display herself for a shilling in a foreign land.

> In another report about the Chinese family, Gilbert à Beckett asks readers to imaginehis Lordship, or any other nobleman, taking out a quantity of upholstery, with his wife and children, and sitting in the 'family of rank' that are honouring us with a long visit – in return for our shillings – at Hyde Park Corner.

à Beckett ridiculed the idea that "mandarins and persons of rank in China" would actually travel to London in order to "condescend to make shows of themselves."[73] The tone of indignation suggests the importance placed on maintaining certain codes of behaviour appropriate to one's social status. à Beckett claimed that "London is beginning to be regularly overrun with Chinese, either genuine or otherwise" and "there ought to be some authority given to detect a counterfeit Chinaman . . . by snipping off his tail, or trying the effect of soap and water on his countenance."[74]

He-Sing, as one of the "counterfeit Chinaman," managed to fool the Queen and Pwan-ye-Koo was reputed to be a "lady of quality," both were considered an affront to established social hierarchies. While the working class in Britain were easily identifiable by mannerisms and dress, He-Sing and Pwan-ye-Koo unsettled social boundaries by masquerading as their "betters" and successfully deceiving the Britons they encountered. Much the same as Cetewayo and George Du Maurier's Japanese man dressed in Western clothing that were discussed in the previous chapter. He-Sing and the Chinese family provoked the ire of the men at *Punch* by not only fooling the Queen and country with apparent ease but also most significantly, by disrupting established social and racial boundaries.

The radical edge that *Punch* provided in the 1840s in their fight for social justice, especially for those most vulnerable in society, started to subside by the 1850s; certainly by the 1860s, the tone and content celebrated "Englishness." The addition of George Du Maurier as a *Punch* staff member in 1864 confirmed the magazine's consistency in providing amusing comments not just on rules of conduct adhered to by the middle and upper classes, but also on the weird absurdities of those who did not belong.[75] Du Maurier provided readers with possibilities of horror when things move beyond their assigned categories. His series of nightmarish cartoons, such as "The Keeper's Nightmare" (Figure 4.12) depicts a selection of fantastical and horrific beasts. Illustrated as a response to the Acclimatisation Society, which promoted the acclimatisation of animals and plants brought to Britain from other countries, the cartoon plays with the idea of animals mixing and breeding, and provides terrifying results of what *could* happen if Britain allows strange intrusions and an acceptance to those who defy assigned categories.[76]

The Great Exhibition introduced British men and women of all classes to ideas of empire by showcasing maps, objects, and human bodies, into a categorisation system.[77] Visitors had the opportunity to see not only manufactured goods on display but also people of diverse races and nations who came to London for the event. These visuals, as exhibition and human displays, blurred the boundary between exhibition and entertainment as well as reality and representation.[78] *Punch*'s reports on the Great Exhibition maintained unified symbols of "Britishness" and created a bond, imagined or otherwise, in which all Britons could identify with. Perceived

FIGURE 4.12 "The Keeper's Nightmare" *Punch Almanack for 1871*, n.p.

Source: Punch, or The London Charivari

shared sense of values and codes of conduct were demarcations that attempted to identify who "we" were while separating those who could never be a part of "us."[79] While light-hearted in tone, *Punch* could "never really rid itself of the accusation that its great shaking of hands was becoming a great shaking of fists"[80] and this "shaking of fists" would become more vigorous during Britain's armed conflict with China in the Second Opium War.

The Second Opium War

Negating China and the Chinese

In January 1857, Tom Taylor wrote for *Punch* a series of letters between Ye Mingchen, acting British Consul Harry Smith Parkes, and other involved British officials during the *Arrow* dispute, which subsequently culminated into the Second Opium War. Hostilities began when Chinese officials, under the direction of Imperial Commissioner Ye boarded a Hong Kong registered vessel named *Arrow* while it was docked in Canton and arrested several of its Chinese crew on suspicion of smuggling. British officials demanded their release and an apology for the insult made to the British flag, to which the Qing officials refused. What resulted was a back-and-forth with Parkes demanding an apology and Ye insisting that there was no insult and therefore no need for an apology.[81] In one of Taylor's satirical letters, Admiral Michael Seymour writes to Parkes, "I am really ashamed to go on pitching into these helpless Chinamen in this style, especially while they are in the right and we in the wrong" and asks, "if I must give them more powder and shot, can't you manage to find me a decent excuse?" In another letter to Parkes, John Bowring, Governor of Hong Kong, declares the war against the Chinese unjustified and concludes, "in an ancient Spartan or a modern Swiss, YEH's conduct might be called heroic. In a Chinaman it is culpably obstinate and cannot be submitted to for a moment."[82]

The letters point to Taylor's sympathies, which lay with China; the satirical letters indicate that Parkes and Bowring were provoking hostilities and Ye was doing his best to find a compromise. This stance would change in the coming weeks as the textual and visual satire created by Taylor and his colleagues at *Punch* sided with Lord Palmerston's war-mongering rhetoric that won over public opinion. Not all the men, however, were in agreement. Douglas Jerrold was a friend of Richard Cobden, the most notable supporter of Ye who strongly opposed the British policy of attacking China.[83] In June 1849, Cobden proposed in the House of Commons the adoption of the principle of arbitration as a means of protesting against violence and massacres, whether at home or abroad. He was defeated but Jerrold wrote fondly of the efforts made by his friend in *Punch*: "the olive twig, planted by Mr. Cobden in Westminster, will flourish despite the blighting wit of mess-rooms, and will rise and spread into a tree that shall offer shade and security for all nations."[84]

In Parliament, Cobden led a long debate with the opposition led by Lord Palmerston, who believed that issues in China were best solved through military action. The "China Question" became a contentious issue and captured the interest of the public. The *Daily News* declared that the "debates on the Canton hostilities have produced a profound impression on the English mind. The moral sense of the country is aroused; the common sense of the country is up in arms."[85] In order to persuade the British people, Palmerston's political rhetoric was laden with stark nationalism; he knew the power of arousing the emotions rather than the intellect of the British people, a lesson he learned during the Don Pacifico affair of 1850. In a famous speech, commended by Prince Albert as a "masterpiece" of rhetoric, Palmerston declared:

> just as a Roman could claim his rights anywhere in the world with the words "*Civis Romanus sum*" ["I am a Roman citizen"], so also a British subject, in whatever land he may be, shall feel confident that the watchful eye and the strong arm of England will protect him against injustice and wrong.[86]

Palmerston hit upon a magic ingredient in appealing to the emotions of the British public through nationalist sentiments in order to garner support. It was not the long and tedious debates that were closely followed by the British public; rather, it was the fervour of nationalist sentiment that Palmerston was successfully able to drum up. In March 1857, Ponny Mayhew characterised the China debate in Parliament as the "Turner Collection" "considering the number of gentlemen who turned their coats on that occasion."[87] It was the astute observations of Taylor and Percival Leigh, however, that accurately accessed the mood of public interest in the China debate. Taylor wrote "Is Lord Palmerston wrong in supporting his subordinates at Canton? Cobden says 'Yeh.' The Country will say 'Nay.'"[88] Leigh put it more bluntly. In a short pun titled "A Tiresome Debate," he wrote that the "Chinese controversy has been altogether a Bo(w)ring discussion."[89] John Wong asserts that the British public had little interest in following the debate in Parliament; instead, he says, "What people wanted was sensation, and Palmerston was going to give them plenty of that."[90]

Palmerston was skilled at manipulating the press, offering journalists, newspaper editors, and proprietors privileged information, access to people, as well as financial bribes in order to secure support at home over his foreign policies.[91] His opponents understood the power in managing the press as well as the interconnection between the press and the public; however, they also realised Palmerston's uncontested mastery in this arena. Cobden wondered,

> How many public men who have ambitions to gratify will range themselves alongside of us so long as the Press is thus opposed to them? To change the Press we must change public opinion. And, mind, when I speak of the Press I speak of those weekly papers which are really supported by the people.[92]

He unsuccessfully attempted to persuade public opinion through the *Morning Star* but his efforts were, quite simply, deemed "anti-British" and therefore made little impact.[93]

It is doubtful that Cobden was surprised by the public reaction. Ten years previously, in an 1847 letter to John Bright, Cobden wrote of the "pugnacious, energetic, self-sufficient, foreigner-despising, and pitying character of the noble insular creature John Bull."[94] In *Punch*, Cobden's political reputation suffered under the magazine's constant attacks. *Punch* equated a vote for Cobden to a vote against England. A "Chinese Election Song" warns that a "vote for COBDEN, DIS, and Co." would "procure PAM's overthrow" and result in a humiliating scenario where "Our fleet [would] retreat" and "JOHN BULL shall do koutou to YEH!"[95]

Punch's shift in tone and attitude towards China and the Chinese became noticeably acrimonious by the end of the Second Opium War and coincided with major London papers that adopted an aggressive stance against China. Only more radical papers argued that "Palmerstonian Mania" was sheer stupidity.[96] Others, such as *The Times*, experienced a change in tone. *The Times* was initially hostile towards Palmerston but this changed by 1855 after John Delane became editor and thought it might be detrimental to the newspaper to be excluded from newsworthy sources. Delane decided to support Palmerston on "his policy upon which the country as a whole was agreed."[97] On 5 January 1857, the newspaper made its stance on "the China Question" by declaring, "the violence and bigotry of local governors was hindering Britain's commercial aims and was the reason for the outbreak of the conflict."[98]

In March 1857, Taylor penned a parody of Alfred Tennyson's *Maud*; the satirical poem, "An Invitation," praises Palmerston. The last stanza reads:

> It is coming, and many a seat
> Is aquake with anxious dread!
> Old Pam they intended to beat,
> But he'll lick them instead.
> Old Pam they intended to beat;
> But England indignant will tread
> Cobden, Dizzy, and Gladstone under her feet,
> And set Pam at the Ministry's head![99]

The laurel accompanies a Large Cut of John Bull sympathetically encouraging a worn-out Palmerston to take a rest in the countryside, away from "those Cobden fellows" (Figure 4.13). In the same volume, Leigh wrote a blatantly nationalistic and xenophobic pun to be sung to the tune of the ballad, *Haul away boys.*[100] The first stanza emphasises Cobden's supposed unpatriotic perspective on the China debate:

> RICHARD COBDEN has a knack,
> Talk away, YEH-O, boys!
> Of hauling down the Union Jack,
> Assailed by any foe, boys.
> Come POPE, come CZAR, come Savage – why
> I know not, still his best he'll try
> To make old England's colours lie
> In degradation low, boys.[101]

FIGURE 4.13 "An Invitation" *Punch*, Vol. 32 (14 March 1857), p. 105.

Source: Punch, or The London Charivari

John Leech's cartoons supported Palmerston's jingoism. His "The Great Chinese Warriors Dah-Bee and Cob-Den" (Figure 4.14) represent Richard Cobden and the Earl of Derby as Chinese warriors. Pro-China was placed in binary opposition to Pro-Britain and the two politicians were represented as fighting for the Chinese and thereby, against the British. The battle cry of "Boh! Hea!" and "Pee! Koe!"

FIGURE 4.14 "The Great Chinese Warriors Dah-Bee and Cob-Den" *Punch*, Vol. 32 (7 March 1857), p. 95.

Source: Punch, or The London Charivari

play on two British favourite Chinese teas and Palmerston is depicted rolling up his sleeve for a fight, visibly un-amused at the possibility of losing his position in Parliament.

More condemnatory is Leech's Large Cut, "A Lesson to John Chinaman." The cartoon depicts Mr. Punch standing alongside Palmerston, holding a cat o'nine tails about to bring down upon a Chinese man with a placard reading "The Destroyer of Women and Children." "Give it him well, Pam, while you are about it!" says Mr. Punch with approval (Figure 4.15). In another half-page cartoon, Palmerston points towards a group of "kidnapping, murdering, poisoning" Chinese, with one man about to throw a baby off a cliff. In the background, buildings are ablaze in a scene of total chaos and Cobden is depicted looking horrified while clutching a statue of Buddha (Figure 4.16). In Parliament, Palmerston attacked Cobden for his "anti-English feeling" and argued that a motion of censure meant that Britain had "abandon a large community of British subjects at the extreme end of the globe to a set of barbarians – a set of kidnapping, murdering, poisoning barbarians."[102] His tactic proved successful; Palmerston won by a majority and Cobden, along with those who supported peace with China, lost their seats for being "un-English."[103]

FIGURE 4.15 "A Lesson to John Chinaman" *Punch*, Vol. 32 (9 May 1857), p. 185.

Source: Punch, or The London Charivari

With Palmerston's majority government, Britain went to war with China. Cobden wrote to Bright, "I consider that we as a nation are little better than brigands, murderers, and poisoners, in our dealings at this moment with half the population of the globe."[104] During the Parliamentary debates, *Punch* began vilifying the Chinese and this negation increased with open hostilities between Britain and China. In February 1857, Jerrold pinpointed the shift towards sinophobia due to the fact that, he claimed, Britons came to "know" the Chinese character:

> The Chinaman has gone down somewhat in the estimation of the thoughtful Briton since GOLDSMITH wrote the *Citizen of the World*. Then, and before then, the Chinese were the most virtuous and the most wonderful of people, because they were utterly unknown. They were painted under the most extravagant forms and in the brightest colours, even as they paint their own china; but even as china becomes flawed and breaks, even so has JOHN CHINAMAN gone, in our opinion, smash. The philanthropist has been found to be as cruel as a cat; the sage has the guile, the petty larceny of a magpie, the man of meekness the obstinacy of a hog. Even as we have sweetened Chinese tea, so have we, of our own liberality, sweetened Chinese character. Let us set aside the saccharine, and judge the pekoe in its native bitterness.[105]

"WHAT CAN YOU SAY FOR YOUR FRIENDS NOW, RICHARD?"

FIGURE 4.16 "What Can You Say for Your Friends Now, Richard?" *Punch*, Vol. 32 (9 May 1857), p. 184.

Source: Punch, or The London Charivari

Shirley Brooks was equally scathing in his assessment. In his report of Parliamentary proceedings, he claimed that

> noble lords who talked of the innocent, polite, and friendly Chinese, had never heard that in Canton itself Mr. Commissioner Yeh had tied up thousands of men and women at this place of execution, and had them flayed alive, and cut into slices.

He noted, "To these people it was urged that we were to serve out 'justice in its most winning guise, and lofty truth and forbearance.'"[106]

In April 1858, Taylor wrote "A Chanson for Canton" to accompany a depiction of a fat Chinese mandarin swaggering across a willow-pattern background with a servant following closely behind (Figure 4.17).

A CHANSON FOR CANTON.

John Chinaman a rogue is born,
The laws of truth he holds in scorn;
About as great a brute as can
Encumber the Earth is John Chinaman.
Sing Yeh, my cruel John Chinaman,
Sing Yeo, my stubborn John Chinaman;
Not Cobden himself can take off the ban
By humanity laid on John Chinaman.

With their little pig-eyes and their large pig-tails,
And their diet of rats, dogs, slugs, and snails,
All seems to be game in the frying-pan
Of that nasty feeder, John Chinaman.
Sing lie-tea, my sly John Chinaman,
No fightee, my coward John Chinaman:
John Bull has a chance—let him, if he can,
Somewhat open the eyes of John Chinaman.

FIGURE 4.17 "A Chanson for Canton" *Punch*, Vol. 34 (10 April 1858), p. 151.

Source: Punch, or The London Charivari

JOHN CHINAMAN a rogue is born,
The laws of truth he holds in scorn;
About as great a brute as can
Encumber the Earth is JOHN CHINAMAN.
Sing YEH, my cruel JOHN CHINAMAN,
Sing YEO, my stubborn JOHN CHINAMAN;
Not COBDEN himself can take off the ban
By humanity laid on JOHN CHINAMAN.

With their little pig-eyes and their large pig-tails,
And their diet of rats, dogs, slugs, and snails,
All seems to be game in the frying-pan
Of that nasty feeder, JOHN CHINAMAN.
Sing lie-tea, my sly JOHN CHINAMAN
No fightee, my coward JOHN CHINAMAN:
JOHN BULL has a chance – let him, if he can,
Somewhat open the eyes of JOHN CHINAMAN.[107]

The Second Opium War was grounded on the idea that Britain was administering "justice" to a savage nation populated by cruel and barbaric people. The viewpoint and criticism of China as a backward civilisation fitted into nineteenth century ideas about progress, society, and history that were expounded by well-respected intellectuals and thinkers of the time. John Stuart Mill believed that the Chinese had "no history" having been "stationary" for thousands of years and "if they are ever to be improved, it must be by foreigners."[108] Palmerston believed that

> These half-civilised governments such as those in China Portugal and Spanish America all require a Dressing every eight or Ten years to keep them in order. Their minds are too shallow to receive an Impression that will last longer than some such Period and warning is of little use. They care little for words and they must not only see the Stick but actually feel it on their Shoulders.[109]

When Lord Elgin arrived in China in 1858, British imperialism was in a fervour following the Sepoy Mutiny in India and a heavy-handed approach was thought needed when up against disobedience.[110] After a series of naval skirmishes, British and French forces seized Guangzhou, captured the unfortunate Ye Mingchen, and started north to secure ratification of the Treaty of Tianjin, which granted the foreign powers all of their demands.[111]

Punch marked the quick victory along with the expected treaty ratifications as an occasion worthy of a Large Cut. In John Tenniel's "A Little Tea Party," the allegorical figures of Britain and France drink gunpowder tea, a British favourite (Figure 4.18). They sit somewhere in China, symbolised by the familiar willow-pattern design on the table and nonsensical "Chinese characters" on the tablecloth.

FIGURE 4.18 "A Little Tea Party" *Punch*, Vol. 35 (4 September 1858), p. 97.

Source: Punch, or The London Charivari

There are holes in the wall, indicating the recent war. Britannia stands with a small canon-shaped teapot and offers a cup to the rotund Chinese Mandarin who looks horrified at the suggestion of more battles with the British. His long, pointed moustache stands on end in comedic theatrical fashion to indicate his alarm. "A little more gunpowder, Mr. China?" asks Britannia. "O-No-Tan-Ke-Mum" replies Mr. China. The message is clear: China had taken enough from the triumphant British.

In June 1859, the British minister in China and Elgin's younger brother, Frederick Bruce, went north to ratify the terms of the Treaty of Tianjin. He sailed "in grand style and the route chosen looked like war"[112] and in response, the Qing government refused his entry into the capital. Bruce responded by opening fire and to the shock of the British and French troops, the Chinese troops fired back killing 519 and wounding 456 British sailors and soldiers.[113] Events quickly escalated; Lord Elgin was once again brought in, more fighting ensued, the British-French troops won the battle, then proceeded to march to Beijing. The Qing court sued for peace but to complicate matters, Harry Parkes and a group under a flag of truce were captured during the conflict and ill-treated, resulting in the death of half of the entourage.[114]

Punch voiced its outrage with John Tenniel's Large Cut titled, "What We Ought to Do in China" (Figure 4.19).[115] The cartoon depicts a British warrior

FIGURE 4.19 "What We Ought to Do in China" *Punch*, Vol. 39 (22 December 1860), p. 245.

Source: Punch, or The London Charivari

on horseback, with ball and chain in hand, he takes aim at a Chinese dragon, which cowers and slinks away. The Chinese are depersonalised and turned into a grotesque creature; reminiscent of the opinions of Mill and Palmerston, China is represented in need of foreign intervention in order to learn to behave in a civil manner. The violent "whipping" that *Punch* advocated was realised; in October 1860, Lord Elgin carried out a punitive mission in which a beautiful complex of palaces called *yuanmingyuan*, known in English as the Summer Palace, was looted and burned to the ground. The Palace was the private property of the Emperor of China and thus Elgin believed that its destruction would be a "blow to his pride as well as his feelings" and "its loss would not be punishment directed at the blameless Chinese people." He posted in public places the cause and reason for the destruction in Chinese as explanation to the Chinese people.[116] Garnet Wolseley, the quartermaster-general for the British contingent, insisted that the only way was to attack the "great vulnerable point in the Mandarin's character: his pride."[117]

Over three days, thousands of men wrought havoc to the palace and its grounds until it lay in devastation.[118] Victor Hugo was horrified at the destruction by Anglo-French forces and famously wrote:

> We Europeans, we are the civilised and for us, the Chinese are the barbarians. This is what civilization has done to barbarism. History will call one of the bandits France and the other England.[119]

Lord Elgin wrote in his diary, "I never felt so ashamed of myself in my life" and sick with depression, he was carried in a sedan chair by sixteen Chinese men to the tune of "God Save the Queen" to the treaty ratification ceremony.[120] Elgin was a fascinating contradictory character that fit well into the paradoxical nature and complicity between imperialism and liberalism that dominated British political thought in the Victorian era. While his early education shaped his beliefs in universal equality and liberty, these notions needed to fluctuate when they came into conflict with the interests of the British Empire.[121]

His mission to China and its catastrophic consequences rekindled memories of Elgin's father, the Seventh Earl of Elgin, who removed the marble sculptures from the Parthenon in Athens half a century earlier.[122] This connection was not lost on *Punch*. Tenniel's "New Elgin Marbles"[123] depicts Lord Elgin standing authoritatively with his new "marbles" (Figure 4.20). The cartoon can be read two ways: Lord Elgin stands with a cannon ball, threatening China to heel or face further violent hostilities; or, Lord Elgin stands with an opium ball, commanding obedience in order to re-establish trade. Either way, one thing is clear in the cartoon and that is China, dehumanised and animalistic, needed both training and supervision by an English master.

In regard to the behaviour of the British and French forces, *Punch*'s reporting gave no indication of sympathy towards China or shock at the destruction of the Summer Palace. The first page of its 1861 publication, "Our Own Correspondent at the Seat of War," serves as an eulogy to Thomas Bowlby, a popular British correspondent for *The Times* and one of the members of Parkes' entourage who did not survive. It references the events concerning the destruction of the Summer Palace in the way Bowlby would have reported, should he still have been alive:

FIGURE 4.20 "New Elgin Marbles" *Punch*, Vol. 39 (24 November 1860), p. 206.

Source: Punch, or The London Charivari

> How eagerly should we have read his description of the Summer Palace, with its glittering fountains, its miles of terraces, its wondrous gardens, and the more than barbaric luxury and glitter within! How vigorously he would have recounted the sack and burning of this fanciful and costly structure! . . . But this was not to be; and just as his tale was awaited here with the greatest expectation, and had aroused the greatest interest, the narrator was struck cruelly down.[124]

There is a clear lack of shock or dismay in the way the British military handled themselves; in fact, the sentiment coincides with Elgin's and Wolseley's belief in the necessity of destruction of the "barbaric luxury" and "fanciful and costly structure" in order to strike at the pride of the Chinese Emperor.

Other reports in *Punch* trivialised the looting and razing of the Summer Palace. Ponny wrote a pun, "Destroying the Enemy's Works" that quipped, "At the sack of the Emperor's Palace at Pekin, a number of valuable watches and clocks were destroyed. We suppose the soldiers did it as an amusement merely by way of killing time."[125] The flippant tone dismissed the devastating wrought upon an architectural wonder and justified the action by portraying the "real" perpetrators of crime as the Chinese. The reduction of such an act to trivial merry-making maintained that there would be no apologies and no regrets.[126] As for Elgin, his return to Britain was greeted with much fan-fare. In January 1861, Brooks' penned a short poetic blurb titled, "A Cheer for Elgin."

> He has done his work featly, adroitly, completely,
> So saith *Mr. Punch*, unaccustomed to flatter;
> And except that the welkin don't rhyme to LORD ELGIN,
> The former should ring with the praise of the latter.[127]

A few months later in April, Brooks' popular "Essence of Parliament" reported, "the victorious ELGIN, home from China, made his appearance, and was cheered by his Peers."[128] Indeed, when Elgin returned to Britain, he discovered that he was aggrandised in public and had become a social and political celebrity.[129]

At the end of the Second Opium War, the British emerged victorious. The terms of the Treaty of Tianjin included the opening of several new ports to Western trade and residence, freedom of movement for Christian missionaries, and the imposition of an enormous indemnity upon China. *Punch* was particularly pleased with the "handsome indemnity" China was obliged to pay.[130] In January 1861, an angry Chinese man kneels in front of a displeased Britannia, offering a sizable willow-patterned teacup piled high with silver taels in "The Real Barbarian From China"[131] (Figure 4.21). The caption references Article 51 in the treaty stipulating that British officials and subjects of the Crown were henceforth outlawed from being referred to as "barbarian," a point of contention that had been building up for some time.

THE REAL BARBARIAN FROM CHINA.

FIGURE 4.21 "The Real Barbarian from China" *Punch*, Vol. 40 (5 January 1861), p. 5.
Source: Punch, or The London Charivari

In James Matheson's 1836 book, *The Present Position and Prospect of Our Trade with China*, he complained that the Chinese used the word *yi* in official documents to refer to the British. Matheson argued that *yi* translated to mean "barbarian" and that its use was insulting to British national honour. It symbolised just how terrible the British were treated by the Chinese and was used as evidence of China's contempt of foreigners, rejection of free trade, and concepts of modern civilisation, thereby hindering the prosperity of British commerce. Matheson used the word *yi* to persuade the British government to go to war with China.[132] The Treaty of Tianjin's Article 51 became the first international treaty to ban a foreign word from its own language.[133]

From the 1840s until the end of the 1860s, *Punch*'s "initial playful seriousness became serious playfulness."[134] References to the Chinese became increasingly venomous, in particular when the magazine decided to vigorously support Palmerston in his campaign for war against China. The radicalism of the early years when *Punch* attempted to be the voice of the poor and powerless and engage in a healthy dose of self-criticism subsided into nationalist sentiments and a belief in Britain's superiority over other nations and races. The Great Exhibition revealed anxieties not just of class and racial disruptions at home, but also reflected wider anxieties of Britain own self-perception and position vis-à-vis the global community. The negative representations of China were therefore important in the production of both a British identity as well as a superior national identity. By 1865, Palmerston was dead, followed five years later by *Punch* editor and co-founder Mark Lemon. From Lemon's death until the end of the Victorian period, three men with different political outlooks took up the position of the editor but the magazine was consistent in its general negation of China and the Chinese. The following chapter will examine how *Punch* used China to both express geopolitical concerns as well as reflect anxieties over Britain's position as a global imperial player.

Notes

1 Name taken from "A Chinese Puzzle" *Punch*, Vol. 21 (1851), p. 19.
2 "The Happy Family in Hyde Park" *Punch*, Vol. 21 (19 July 1851), p. 36.
3 Auerback, *The Great Exhibition of 1851*, p. 159.
4 Edward Ziter, *The Orient on the Victorian Stage* (Cambridge: Cambridge University Press, 2003), p. 107.
5 Anne Veronica Witchard, *Thomas Burke's Dark "Chinoiserie": Limehouse Nights* and the Queer Spell of Chinatown (Farnham, UK: Ashgate Publishing Limited, 2009), p. 42.
6 Richard D. Altick, *The Shows of London* (Cambridge, MA: Belknap Press, 1978), p. 292.
7 William B. Langdon, London's curator for the show, extended the original catalogue titled *Ten Thousand Chinese Things,* to include commentaries from China experts and sold more than three hundred thousand copies of which there were several editions between 1842 and 1844. See Pagani, "Objects and the Press," pp. 150–151.
8 Altick, *The Shows of London*, p. 335.
9 Witchard, *Thomas Burke's Dark "Chinoiserie,"* p. 42.
10 Altick, *The Shows of London*, p. 335.
11 Pagani, "Chinese Material Culture and British Perceptions of China in the Mid-Nineteenth Century," p. 35.
12 Nathan Dunn and William B. Langdon, *"Ten Thousand Chinese Things": A Descriptive Catalogue of the Chinese* (London, England, 1843), p. 14.
13 *Illustrated London News*, No. 13 (6 August 1842), pp. 204–205.
14 "The Chinese Exhibition at Knightsbridge" *Punch*, Vol. 3 (1842), p. 197.
15 *Punch's Guide to the Chinese Exhibition at Knightsbridge* (London, 1842), p. 12, p. 31.
16 "The Chinese Exhibition at Knightsbridge" *Punch* Vol. 3 (1842), p. 196.
17 James L. Hevia, *Cherishing Men from Afar* (Durham; London: Duke University Press, 1995), pp. 73–74.
18 Blue, "China and Western Social Thought in the Modern Period," p. 73.
19 "Punch Among the Celestials" *Punch*, Vol. 15 (1848), p. 12.
20 *London Illustrated News* (29 August 1851), p. 148, p. 179.
21 Hector Berlioz, *Evenings With the Orchestra,* translated by Jacques Barzun (New York: Alfred A. Knopf, 1956), pp. 246–250.
22 Altick, *The Shows of London*, p. 463.
23 "The Peace with China" *Punch*, Vol. 3 (1842), p. 237.
24 "The Queen's Speech – Peace with China" *Punch*, Vol. 3 (1842), p. 56.
25 Witchard, *Thomas Burke's Dark "Chinoiserie,"* p. 55.
26 Samuel Phillips Day, *Tea: Its Mystery and History* (London: Simpin, Marshall & Co., 1878), p. 71.
27 Day, *Tea*, p. 70.
28 John Burnett, *Plenty & Want: A Social History of Diet in England From 1815 to the Present Day* (London: Scolar Press, 1979), diet of poor labourers, p. 17; consumption of tea per annum per head, p. 131.
29 Burnett, *Plenty & Want*, p. 132.
30 "The Peace with China" *Punch*, Vol. 3 (1842), p. 237.

31 *Punch* was not alone in their use of satirical wit to criticise Britain's desire for a free market economy in China. *The Comic Album: A Book for Every Table* of 1842 published a satirical poem titled "The Chinese War" that was later re-published in the *Illustrated London News* of 10 December 1842: "With this nation so deluded/Peace is happily concluded:/Let us now no longer teaze/The unfortunate Chinese./We are ready to befriend them;/Cotton night-gowns we will send them;/For their use we will import/ Articles of every sort . . . /Everything, in fact, to please/And enlighten the Chinese,/ England, this time forth supplies them./Only just to civilize them." See "The Chinese War" *The Comic Album: A Book for Every Table* (London: Orr and Co., 1842) cited in Pagani "Objects and the Press" p. 149; Pagani, "Chinese Material Culture" p. 32.
32 "Peace with the Pig-Tails" *Punch*, Vol. 3 (1842), p. 238.
33 Dominic Janes, "The Role of Visual Appearance in Punch's Early Victorian Satires on Religion" *Victorian Periodicals Review*, Vol. 47, No. 1 (Spring 2014), pp. 67–68.
34 "Business and The Bayonet" *Punch*, Vol. 19 (1850), p. 234.
35 The plight of needlewomen has been a *Punch* cause over numerous years. Victorian needlewomen were usually uneducated and without family support. Their low pay and appalling work and living conditions shocked the public and resulted in many short stories, plays, and poetry – the most famous being Thomas Hood's "The Song of the Shirt" first published in *Punch* in December 1843. For more on the Victorian needlewomen, see Beth Harris, "'Slaves of the Needle': The Seamstress in the 1840s" (14 December 2014), *The Victorian Web*. Online: http://www.victorianweb.org/gender/ugoretz1.html.
36 Matthewson, "Satirising Imperial Anxiety in Victorian Britain," pp. 9–13.
37 Auerback, *The Great Exhibition of 1851,* p. 1.
38 Message and Johnston, "The World Within the City," pp. 33–34.
39 Diana J. Reynolds, "The Great Exhibition of 1851 – Interpretive Essay" *Events That Changed Great Britain Since 1689* (eds.) Frank W. Thackeray and John E. Findling (Westport, CT; London: Greenwood, 2002), p. 100.
40 Frederick William of Prussia to the Prince Consort, 8 April 1851, Royal Archives Commissioners Records in the custody of the Royal Commission for the Exhibition of 1851, Lowther Gardens, London, cited in Audrey Short, "Workers Under Glass in 1851" *Victorian Studies*, Vol. 10, No. 2 (December 1966), p. 193.
41 Jeffrey Auerbach, "The Great Exhibition and Historical Memory" *Journal of Victorian Culture*, Vol. 6, No. 1 (2001), p. 102.
42 The Exhibition was from May to October 1851 and the admission fee dropped further over the course of the exhibition. To put the pricing in perspective, Auerback references "the skilled laborers at the Crystal Palace [who] were paid on average 28s a week." See Auerback, *The Great Exhibition of 1851*, pp. 145–146.
43 There were several ways that classes segregated themselves. The trains coming into London from various northern industrial areas had a strict division of coaches into first, second, and third classes. Another example is the opening ceremony of the Great Exhibition, which the Royal Commission made a decision to exclude the public. For Lord Palmerston, see Auerback, *The Great Exhibition of 1851,* p. 158. For division on trains, see Clive Behagg, *Labour and Reform: Working Class Movements 1815–1914* (London: Hodder and Stoughton, 1991), pp. 76–78, cited in Steve Edwards, "The Accumulation of Knowledge or, William Whewell's Eye" *The Great Exhibition of 1851: New Interdisciplinary Essays* (ed.) Louise Purbick (Manchester; New York: Manchester University Press, 2001), p. 29. For the Royal Commission's decision, see Peter Gurney, "An Appropriated Space: The Great Exhibition, the Crystal Palace and the Working Class" *The Great Exhibition of 1851: New Interdisciplinary Essays* (ed.) Louise Purbick (Manchester; New York: Manchester University Press, 2001), p. 119.
44 Auerback, *The Great Exhibition of 1851*, p. 139.
45 Auerback, *The Great Exhibition of 1851*, p. 155.
46 Auerback, *The Great Exhibition of 1851*, p. 154.
47 John Tallis, *Tallis's History and Description of the Crystal Palace, and the Exhibition of the World's Industry in 1851* (London; New York: J. Tallis and Co., 1851), Vol. 1, p. 102.

48 Gideon Mantell, *The Journal of Gideon Mantell*, edited by E. Cecil Curwen (London: Oxford University Press, 1940), pp. 273–274.

49 The Great Exhibition catering to the middle and upper classes is exemplified by the prize medals awarded at the event. The medals were inscribed in Latin, a language only understood by the elite and in most cases, they were awarded to the entrepreneurs and not the workers who actually produced the exhibit. See Auerback, *The Great Exhibition of 1851*, p. 133; and, Gurney, "An Appropriated Space," pp. 114–145.

50 Reynolds, "The Great Exhibition of 1851 – Interpretive Essay," p. 101.

51 Adina Ciugureanu, "Mediating Between the Mass and the Individual: *Punch* Caricatures of the Great Exhibition of All Nations" *Gramma: Journal of Theory and Criticism*, Vol. 18 (2010), p. 110.

52 *The Crystal Palace and Its Contents; Being an Illustrated Cyclopaedia of the Great Exhibition of the Industry of All Nations* (London: W.M. Clark, 1852), p. 100, cited in Paul Young, "Mission Impossible: Globalization and the Great Exhibition" *Britain, the Empire, and the World at the Great Exhibition of 1851* (eds.) Jeffrey A. Auerbach and Peter H. Hoffenberg (London & New York: Ashgate Publishing, 2008), p. 17.

53 *The Times* (8 October 1851) cited in Auerback, *The Great Exhibition of 1851*, p. 158.

54 Cobden was speaking at a public meeting in Birmingham. Cited in Auerback, *The Great Exhibition of 1851*, p. 163. In reality, how many foreigners actually attended the event is questionable. *Punch* makes note of this in an article titled, "Where Are the Foreigners?" See *Punch*, Vol. 20 (1851), p. 207.

55 Cited in Banta, *Barbaric Intercourse*, p. 93.

56 Auerback, *The Great Exhibition of 1851*, pp. 181–182.

57 "The Year of Expectations" *Punch*, Vol. 20 (1851), p. 104.

58 Auerbach, *The Great Exhibition of 1851*, p. 176.

59 Louise Tythacott, *The Lives of Chinese Objects* (New York: Berghahn Books, 2011), pp. 87–88.

60 Louise Purbrick, "Introduction" *The Great Exhibition of 1851: New Interdisciplinary Essays* (ed.) Louise Purbick (Manchester & New York: Manchester University Press, 2001), p. 8.

61 John R. Davis, *The Great Exhibition* (Stroud: Sutton Publishing, 1999), p. 105. Tythacott also claims that China emerged as the "antithesis of the country that hosted the Exhibition" in Tythacott, *The Lives of Chinese Objects*, p. 83.

62 The Chinese nationalist, Zou Rong brought attention to the British laughing at the Chinese hairstyle in 1903 in *The Revolutionary Army*. He asks "When a man with a queue and wearing Manchu clothes wanders around London, why do all the passers-by say 'Pig-tail' or 'Savage'?" See Michael R. Godley "The End of the Queue: Hair as Symbol in Chinese History" *China Heritage Quarterly*, No. 27 (September 2011). Online: http://www.chinaheritagequarterly.org.

63 Francesca Vanke, "Degrees of Otherness: The Ottoman Empire and China at the Great Exhibition of 1851" *Britain, the Empire, and the World at the Great Exhibition of 1851* (eds.) Jeffrey A. Auerbach and Peter H. Hoffenberg (Aldershot, England; Burlington, VT: Ashgate Publishing Ltd., 2008), p. 203. Witchard notes that "Westerners perceived the pigtails of Chinese men as an utter absurdity" in Witchard, *Thomas Burke's Dark 'Chinoiserie'*, p. 81.

64 "London Dining Rooms, 1851" *Punch Almanack for 1851*, Vol. 20, n.p.

65 Davis and Tythacott draw attention to the respect shown to He-Sing when it was believed that he was a foreign representative at the event; thus, being Chinese did not afford him any less respect as would be shown other foreign dignitaries. Edmund Yates recorded events and claimed that He-Sing "being mistaken for a grandee, was received with the greatest honour, and had one of the best places in the show." Davis, *The Great Exhibition*, p. 130; Tythacott, *The Lives of Chinese Objects*, p. 89; on Edmund Yates, see *Edmund Yates,* His Recollections and Experiences, 1885, in particular chapter on 1847–1852, cited in "Victorian London – Entertainment and Recreation – Museums, Public Buildings and Galleries – The Chinese Collection / Chinese Exhibition" on *The Victorian Dictionary: Exploring Victorian London*. Online: http://www.victorianlondon.org/entertainment/chinesecollection.htm.

66 Reports differ on He-Sing's role on the *Keying*; some reports claim he is the proprietor of the junk while others claim he was only a sailor. Auerbach, *The Great Exhibition of 1851*, p. 178; On varying reports of He-Sing, see Witchard, *Thomas Burke's Dark 'Chinoiserie'*, pp. 44–51, in particular p. 51; Tythacott, *The Lives of Chinese Objects*, p. 89; Altick, *The Shows of London*, p. 460.

67 Letter to Mrs. Brookfield, 1 May 1851, *The Letters and Private Papers of William Makepeace Thackeray* (ed.) Gordon N. Ray (London: Oxford University Press, 1945), Vol. 3, p. 768, cited in Witchard, *Thomas Burke's Dark "Chinoiserie,"* p. 51.

68 "Punch's Own Report of the Opening of the Great Exhibition" *Punch*, Vol. 20 (10 May 1851), p. 190.

69 Hevia, *English Lessons*, pp. 63–65.

70 He-Sing's appearance may have inspired Henry Sutherland Edwards's satirical booklet, *An account of the Chinese commission which was sent to report on the Great Exhibition.* The work is a long, rhyming poem telling the story of the Emperor of China who sent two delegates to the Great Exhibition to report on what they saw. Auerbach states that the booklet is an obvious example of the orientalist impulse to denigrate a race in order to highlight the positive values of Britain. Tythacott sees the work as a document that represents a deep hostility towards China and reflects the xenophobic tendencies of the Exhibition. Witchard argues that Edwards's booklet is a type of Sino-satire made for readers to have a laugh at their own society's shortcomings. See Auerbach, *The Great Exhibition of 1851*, pp. 174–179; Tythacott, *The Lives of Chinese Objects*, pp. 89–91; Witchard, *Thomas Burke's Dark 'Chinoiserie'*, pp. 44–46.

71 "The Chinese Family" *Illustrated London News* (24 May 1851), p. 13.

72 "A Chinese Puzzle" *Punch*, Vol. 21 (1851), p. 19.

73 "The Chinese in London" *Punch*, Vol. 21 (23 August 1851), p. 86.

74 "The Chinese in London" *Punch*, Vol. 21 (23 August 1851), p. 86.

75 Banta, *Barbaric Intercourse*, pp. 74–75.

76 Banta, *Barbaric Intercourse*, pp. 80–88.

77 Auerbach, *The Great Exhibition of 1851*, pp. 101–102.

78 Ziter, *The Orient on the Victorian Stage*, p. 3.

79 Banta, *Barbaric Intercourse*, p. 34.

80 Richard Pearson, "Thackeray and *Punch* at the Great Exhibition: authority and ambivalence in verbal and visual caricatures" *The Great Exhibition of 1851: New Interdisciplinary Essays* (ed.) Louise Purbick (Manchester & New York: Manchester University Press, 2001), p. 188.

81 Robert Bickers, *The Scramble for China: Foreign Devils in the Qing Empire, 1832–1914* (London: Allen Lane, 2011), pp. 136–150.

82 "About the English of It" *Punch*, Vol. 32 (24 January 1857), pp. 32–33.

83 Cobden was supported by William Gladstone, Earl of Derby, Lord John Russell, and Benjamin Disraeli, among others.

84 "Peace and War in Parliament" *Punch*, Vol. 16 (23 June 1849), p. 257.

85 "The China Question" *Daily News* (2 March 1857), p. 4.

86 The Don Pacifico affair of 1850, in which David Pacifico, a British Jew born in Gibraltar but residing in Athens asked for the protection of the British government after he was attacked by an anti-Semitic mob. Palmerston supported Pacifico and sent the navy to blockade the Greek coast against the protests of other European nations. Cobden disagreed with this sign of aggression. While the affair did not alter the course of British foreign policy, Palmerston succeeded in arousing an emotive sense of nationalism in British popular politics by comparing the British and Roman empires. See Auerbach, *The Great Exhibition of 1851*, pp. 164–165; Geoffrey Hicks, "Don Pacifico, Democracy, and Danger: The Protectionist Party Critique of British Foreign Policy, 1850–1852" *The International History Review*, Vol. 26, No. 3 (September 2004), pp. 515–540; Basil Kingsley Martin, *The Triumph of Lord Palmerston* (London: G. Allen & Unwin, 1924), pp. 51–66.

87 "Turner's Collection" *Punch*, Vol. 32 (14 March 1857), p. 107.
88 "A Prophecy" *Punch*, Vol. 32 (14 March 1857), p. 107.
89 "A Tiresome Debate" *Punch*, Vol. 32 (14 March 1857), p. 108.
90 J. Y. Wong, *Deadly Dreams: Opium, Imperialism and the 'Arrow' War (1856–60) in China* (Cambridge: Cambridge University Press, 1998), pp. 235–246; Brown, "Diplomacy and the Fourth Estate," p. 225.
91 Brown, "Diplomacy and the Fourth Estate," pp. 41–43.
92 Cited in Basil Kingsley Martin, *The Triumph of Lord Palmerston* (London: G. Allen & Unwin, 1924), p. 49. Cobden was speaking about violence abroad and not about war with China specifically.
93 Brown, "Diplomacy and the Fourth Estate," pp. 43–44.
94 Cited in Martin, *The Triumph of Lord Palmerston*, p. 48.
95 "Chinese Election Song" *Punch*, Vol. 32 (28 March 1857), p. 123.
96 Wong, *Deadly Dreams*, pp. 235–246; Brown, "Diplomacy and the Fourth Estate," p. 44.
97 Wong, *Deadly Dreams*, pp. 154–155.
98 *The Times* (5 January 1857), p. 6.
99 "An Invitation" *Punch*, Vol. 32 (14 March 1857), p. 104.
100 A sea shanty written by Thomas Dibdin (1771–1841), "Haul Away Boys" Bodleian Libraries, Harding B25 (812), Ballad – Roud Number V21062, Broadside Ballads Online, ballads.bodleian.ox.ac.uk/view/sheet/4370. The ballad begins with the first line "British sailors have a knack."
101 "Cobden's Capability" *Punch*, Vol. 32 (14 March 1857), p. 101.
102 "Henry John Temple, 3rd Viscount Palmerston: Arrow Controversy and the Second Opium War" *New World Encyclopedia*. Online: www.newworldencyclopedia.org/entry/Henry_John_Temple,_3rd_Viscount_Palmerston.
103 Julia Lovell, *The Opium War* (London: Picador, 2011), pp. 255–256.
104 Cited in H. Donaldson Jordan, "The Case of Richard Cobden" *Proceedings of the Massachusetts Historical Society*, Third Series, Vol. 83 (1971), p. 38.
105 "A Few Mandarins Wanted" *Punch*, Vol. 32 (14 February 1857), p. 70.
106 "Punch's Essence of Parliament" *Punch*, Vol. 32 (7 March 1857), p. 91.
107 "A Chanson for Canton" *Punch*, Vol. 34 (10 April 1858), p. 151.
108 John Stuart Mill cited in Blue, "China and Western Social Thought in the Modern Period," p. 77. For a detailed discussion on Mill thoughts on China as a stagnant nation, see Michael Levin, *J.S. Mill on Civilization and Barbarism* (London: Routledge, 2004), in particular Chapter Six, "Standstill: The Case of China," pp. 94–120.
109 Palmerston, autograph note, 29 September 1850 (F.O. 17/173), cited in Blue, "China and Western Social Thought in the Modern Period," p. 77; and cited in Levin, *J.S. Mill on Civilization and Barbarism*, p. 103.
110 Bickers, *The Scramble for China*, p. 145; Witchard, *Thomas Burke's Dark "Chinoiserie,"* p. 65.
111 Bickers, *The Scramble for China*, pp. 146–147; Lovell, *The Opium War*, pp. 258–259.
112 Bickers, *The Scramble for China*, p. 148.
113 Lovell states that 519 were killed and 456 wounded; Hevia claims there were "434 casualties including 89 dead." Lovell, *The Opium War*, p. 259; Hevia, *English Lessons*, p. 40.
114 Bickers, *The Scramble for China*, pp. 148–149.
115 "What We Ought to do in China" *Punch*, Vol. 39 (22 December 1860), p. 245.
116 Hevia, *English Lessons*, pp. 106–107.
117 Hevia, *English Lessons*, p. 111.
118 Bickers, *The Scramble for China*, pp. 149–150; Lovell, *The Opium War*, pp. 262–266.
119 "*Nous, Européens, nous sommes les civilises, et pour nous, les Chinois sont les barbares. Voila ce que la civilisation a fait à la barbarie. Devant l'histoire, l'un des deux bandits s'appellera la France, l'autre s'appellera L'Angleterre.*" Translation mine. "Victor Hugo et le Sac du Palais

D'Été" *Le Monde Diplomatique*, octobre 2004, p. 18. Online: https://www.mode-diplomatique.fr/2004/10/HUGO/11563.
120 Witchard, *Thomas Burke's Dark 'Chinoiserie'*, p. 66; Lovell, *The Opium War*, p. 265; Hevia, *English Lessons*, pp. 114–115.
121 Q. S. Tong, "Traveling Imperialism: Lord Elgin's Missions to China and the Limits of Victorian Liberalism" *A Century of Travels in China* (eds.) Douglas Kerr and Julia Kuehn (Hong Kong: Hong Kong University Press, 2007), pp. 45–46.
122 Tong, "Traveling Imperialism," p. 45.
123 "New Elgin Marbles" *Punch*, Vol. 39 (24 November 1860), p. 206.
124 "Our Own Correspondent at the Seat of War" *Punch*, Vol. 40 (5 January 1861), p. 1.
125 "Destroying the Enemy's Works" *Punch*, Vol. 40 (12 January 1861), p. 22.
126 Hevia, *English Lessons*, p. 111.
127 "A Cheer for Elgin" *Punch*, Vol. 40 (5 January 1861), p. 3.
128 "*Punch*'s Essence of Parliament" *Punch*, Vol. 40 (20 April 1861), p. 161.
129 Tong, "Traveling Imperialism," p. 50.
130 Spielmann, *The History of "Punch,"* p. 119.
131 "The Real Barbarian from China" *Punch*, Vol. 40 (5 January 1861), p. 5.
132 Lydia H. Liu, "The Thug, the Barbarian, and the Work of Imperial Warfare" *Modern Language Association*, Vol. 124, No. 5 (October 2009), p. 1860; Song-Chuan Chen, *Merchants of War and Peace* (Hong Kong: Hong Kong University Press, 2017), in particular Chapter 5, pp. 82–102.
133 Liu, "The Thug, the Barbarian, and the Work of Imperial Warfare," p. 1861.
134 Banta, *Barbaric Intercourse*, p. 59.

5

"A LEGACY OF DISCORD"[1]

War and rebellion

John Tenniel's "A Touching Appeal" depicts an overgrown childlike Chinese man named Younghy-Bung-Boo-Hoo who starts a fight but then loses to a much smaller Japanese man (Figure 5.1). The Japanese figure stands strong and ready for action; both hands are clenched into fists and he leans threateningly towards the defeated Younghy-Bung-Boo-Hoo who sits on the ground, his nose red as a result from the fight. Edwin Milliken's accompanying "poem" explains the cartoon. The "proud" Younghy-Bung-Boo-Hoo was "jealous of a Jappy," who, although small, was a "plucky chappie/[and] Made big Younghy feel unhappy." The animosity resulted in a physical confrontation where Younghy, "the big boy pale and yellow," was quickly defeated and "began to bleat and bellow." Being "fearful for his life," he cried out, "Though you welly lilly body, Jap, you strikee biggy blow! Welly much hurtee – me no play!!" His Japanese opponent shows no mercy "And he cried 'Fight on, man, *do!*'" and tells his Chinese rival, "Yah! In fighting I'm your mate. /You cave in a bit too late, /I will whop you – if you'll wait."[2] The poem ends with Younghy-Bung-Boo-Hoo whinging that the foreigners, who are standing watch in the background, do nothing to help.

This cartoon and accompanying "poem" was published in November 1894, during the First Sino-Japanese war, a conflict between China and Japan over supremacy in Korea. It was a short but decisive war and the consequences were paramount in shifting the balance of world power. Western powers were astounded by China's rapid defeat and theorised that this was the result of China's extensive corruption, stubborn resistance to Western technology, and the nation's backwardness. Japan emerged as a new imperial player on the international arena and "A Touching Appeal" reflected this shift in power. The message in the cartoon declared that China may be great in size but it is not great in strength. Japan, on

DOI: 10.4324/9781003025573-5

FIGURE 5.1 "A Touching Appeal" *Punch*, Vol. 107 (17 November 1894), p. 235.

Source: Punch, or The London Charivari

the other hand, is represented in relatable terms; not only is it an island nation like Britain, but also the Japanese are characterised as people with plucky spirits, a trait easily identifiable as it is found in the emblematic John Bull, who embodies pugnacity, independence, and courage.[3]

Milliken's "poem" is equally significant as it is within this textual representation that China and Japan are categorised and understood within the British popular imagination. Younghy speaks in broken pidgin English and his rival, the Japanese man, communicates in standard, grammatically correct English. For the Chinese, the use of "pidgin," a derivative of the English word for "business," was taken seriously as it was considered a valuable tool needed in order to engage in the lucrative trade sector.[4] Europeans and Americans, however, viewed pidgin English as something laughable and it was associated with non-Caucasians with low social status.[5] This perception combined with the difficulty the Chinese have in pronouncing some consonants resulted in pidgin being frequently employed for comedic effect and this had a "profound impact on popular perception."[6] The Japanese were also subjected to ridicule in their use of Yokohama Pidgin. For example, Hoffman Atkinson poked fun of its use in his humorous pamphlet, *Exercises in the Yokohama Dialect* published in Yokohama and then reviewed by C.G. Leland in London's *New Quarterly Magazine* in 1879.[7] "A Touching Appeal" is notable in focusing linguistic humour solely on the Chinese figure and this is significant.

The Victorian era was a time when dictionaries and grammars were emphasising norms and rules for how the English language should, and should not, be used and the writers at *Punch* prided themselves at using humour to "defend" the English language against abuse and debasement. Appropriate use was set as a crucial marker that separated the cultivated middle class from the rustic working class. There was therefore a "right" and "wrong" way to speak English and *Punch* staff members "recognized that the proper use of language was vital to the image of middle-class respectability."[8] This distinction was all-the more pronounced when the use of English was employed to accentuate "foreignness." Tenniel's Japanese figure with command of the English language "signified full cultural competence and social prestige" and indicated that Japan was able to enter the "civilised" world.[9] The Chinese, on the other hand, were not able to successfully integrate themselves into the modern world and were thus represented as inferior speakers.

This chapter explores *Punch*'s engagement with turn-of-the century imperialist discourse. Events in China during the 1890s generated much interest and *Punch* not only interacted with new developments of imperialism but also contributed to particular notions and ideas of China and Japan in the British imagination. The admiration of Japan as a plucky nation entering the international arena as a formidable power in "A Touching Appeal" quickly dissipated into anxieties over British interests in China. As the nineteenth century came to a close, *Punch* redirected its focus on the fractured alliances and increased tensions between imperial rivals who joined forces to suppress the Boxer Uprising. With Britain's heightened geopolitical awareness and conscientiousness in its global political and economic position, *Punch* used its cartoons as a powerful tool to justify Britain's presence in China as well as convince its readers of nations they should regard with suspicion.

The first Sino-Japanese war

The shift in geopolitics

In 1894, with war between China and Japan imminent, Sir Robert Hart, Inspector-General of China's Imperial Maritime Custom declared "999 out of every 1000 Chinese are sure big China can thrash little Japan."[10] Hart, however, did not have the benefit of hindsight and could not have considered the complications surrounding China such as the disastrous mismanagement of military funds,[11] the shortage of much needed ammunition to supply the Chinese army,[12] the failure of Chinese leadership, as well as China's lack of understanding of the importance of Japan's modernisation reforms, and what that meant in relation to the Manchu-ruled country.[13] At the outbreak of hostilities, all eyes were on unfolding events. The war generated a great deal of interest and many believed that China had a strong, modern navy with well-built forts and even if the army was not yet fully trained, the sheer numbers would certainly "turn the scale in her favour."[14]

News media from around the globe reported on events with the London *Times* providing the most detailed coverage.[15] Before long, Western journalists noticed and started complaining of irregularities and inaccuracies in the news stories printed by both the Chinese and the Japanese press. In September 1894, *The Pall Mall Gazette* published an article condemning the misreporting of the war:Those who may have been in doubt as to whether the art of lying is in a state of decay should have had that doubt removed by reading the various accounts of the fight at the Yalu, at any rate, as far as the East is concerned. There is a finished effrontery about the telegrams which shows that both sides are splendid liars.[16]

A month later, the newspaper explained to readers why it thought there were erroneous reports, "The reason why the war news is so woefully inaccurate is to be found in the fact that not a solitary European correspondent is permitted to the front by either of the belligerents."[17]

Punch joined the sense of outrage by the misinformation on events surrounding the war. In September 1894, Milliken quipped that there are "Wild contradictions and vagueness extreme, /Faith, it all reads like Flowery Land dream."[18] Arthur à Beckett went further in February 1895 in "Toning It Down." The article is divided into two sections, one for the Japanese version of events and the other for the Chinese. Both claim that during a particular battle, which remains unnamed, their respective side was victorious. The Japanese claim that only "a cabin-boy [was] wounded. The Chinese prisoners amounted to 180,000 men" whereas the Chinese claim that the "slaughter of the Japs was enormous, amounting to at least 40,000 sailors and 50,000 marines. There was no loss on the Chinese side."[19] With Japan emerging victorious battle after battle, the Japanese government decided to allow foreign correspondents to accompany the Japanese army. This decision was most welcomed; the observations reported by white men permitted on the scene were considered both reliable and trustworthy by the Western press.[20] By contrast, foreign journalists were not allowed to accompany the Chinese military.

Japan was quick to grasp the importance of representation. For example, Japanese woodblock print artists paid close attention in their depictions of the Japanese army with modern uniforms and the latest weapons. These images contrasted starkly with their representations of the Chinese military in traditional attire equipped with outdated weapons. Japan not only played the part of a civilised nation in adopting Western technological achievements but they also *looked* like a unified, trained, military apparatus and this was significant in winning the war of perceptions among the global community. Japan understood that modern-style uniforms were a visual display of modernity and progress; to the Chinese, they simply viewed Japan's adoption as nothing more than mimicry.[21] Japan was also careful to fight a "civilised" war in accordance with Western standards to demonstrate to the world that it had become a modern, industrialised power.[22] The major exception occurred in November 1894 when Japanese troops, after seeing the mutilated bodies of their military comrades, inflicted a three-day slaughter on the defeated population at Port Arthur.

Thomas Cowan of the *Times* witnessed the fall of Port Arthur. The first day of the capture, Cowan excused the Japanese army but reported to be "greatly surprised next day to find them still killing the Chinese." While he supported the Japanese claims that it was difficult to discern between soldiers and civilians, he said that this did not explain the summary execution of women and children and conjectured that the Japanese "also are barbarous at heart, like the Chinese."[23] Another witness, James Allan wrote a book about the war and justified the massacre at Port Arthur by claiming, "Strongly as the massacre by the Japanese troops in Port Arthur is to be condemned, there is not the slightest doubt in the world that the Chinese brought it on themselves by their own vindictive savagery towards their enemies."[24] The British war correspondent Frederic Villiers felt differently. He writes that the Japanese army, upon seeing the horrific remains of their comrades, provided "almost an excuse for the conduct of the troops [on the first day], but that the last two days' work might carry another term" and after considering what the term should be, he writes that it is "called . . . a cold-blooded butchery. It was a cold-blooded butchery."[25]

In January 1895, Milliken condemned the brutality of the Japanese army in "A Gentle Hint to the Jubilant Jap" that highlighted the battles won before ending with:

> But, though their pluck be grand,
> Bar-bar-i-ty
> Their choicest gifts will mar,
> Blood stains their rising star,
> Foul slaughter is not war.
> Fie, Jappy, fie![26]

The denunciation was one of the only serious comments found in *Punch* pertaining to the Sino-Japanese war; instead, the magazine tended to reduce the horrors and violence of war to a series of cute and comical events using familiar nursery rhymes. Tenniel employed the legendary story of David and Goliath to depict a boisterous, pint-sized Japan giving the giant, China, a good walloping. As the cover-art for *Punch* volume 107, Mr. Punch watches behind a fence at an exuberant, and tiny, Japanese man bravely approaching a Chinese giant (Figure 5.2).[27] Within the magazine, Tenniel's Large Cut cartoon, "Jap the Giant

FIGURE 5.2 "Front page" *Punch*, Vol. 107 (11 August 1894), n.p.

Source: Punch, or The London Charivari

Killer," depicts a tiny Japanese soldier stands on top of a bewildered looking Chinese giant, laying on his back with legs kicking in an unsuccessful attempt to pick himself up (Figure 5.3).

Milliken provided a story to accompany Tenniel's cartoons. The story describes the hatred between Japan (named "Little Jap") and China (named "Big Jon-ni") and indeed, Big Jon-ni "disdained everybody else save his conceited and colossal self." It explains that Big Jon-ni has been "in a state of abstraction for nine centuries" and in this static state, he "lost the use of his head, as well as his legs! He hates and scorns [Japan's] tutelary goddess, Pro-Gress."[28] The opinion that China was losing the war due to self-imposed stagnation was shared by reports in *The Times*, *Punch*'s preferred media outlet for its news stories. On 26December 1894, *The Times* claimed that with

> passionate effort the Japanese have ransacked the Western world for its treasures of knowledge, and have vigorously applied what they have learned. The Chinese, on the other hand, have set their face against the science of other nations, and, with an unhappy mixture of apathy and contempt, have rejected the teaching which has been pressed upon them.[29]

In another Large Cut, Linley Sambourne drew what he called in his diary, "China Boy & Japanese Bee."[30] The cartoon depicts a little Chinese boy named Ah Sid

FIGURE 5.3 "Jap the Giant-Killer" *Punch*, Vol. 107 (29 September 1894), p. 151.

Source: Punch, or The London Charivari

FIGURE 5.4 "Little Ah Sid and the Butterfly-Bee" *Punch*, Vol. 107 (20 October 1894), p. 182.

Source: Punch, or The London Charivari

(acid), who has thrown his bow and arrow to the ground as he runs from a determined little bee, ready to physically chastise the boy with a small baton (Figure 5.4).

Milliken once again provides an accompanying text explaining that Ah Sid "was fond of his fun" and while he was at play, he spotted a Japanese bumblebee. In "malice secure," Ah Sid chased the bee in order to pull off its wings. To his great surprise, the bumblebee fights back and the poem finishes with Ah Sid getting his comeuppance with a sting from the bee. Reminiscent of Aesop's fable, *The Ant and the Grasshopper*, Ah Sid prefers to idle away his time in "fun" and "frolics" and his "pig-headed" ways resulted in an industrious Japanese bumblebee entering Ah Sid's territory and stinging him where it hurts most, which was China's loss of territory, regional power, and international status.

Punch continually poked fun at the idea of a small nation like Japan defeating an enormous China, but there were deeper significations within the cartoons and textual accompaniments. The combination of words and images reflected an important change not only in the dynamics between China and Japan, but also of Japan's elevated international status and subsequent shift of geopolitical power. Arthur Diósy, founder of the Japan Society of the United Kingdom, explained the new global balance of power:

> Governments that had, in the past, treated Japan with scant courtesy, now seriously considered the question of an alliance with her. Other great Powers paid her the almost equally great compliment of looking upon her as a dangerous rival . . . Friends and foes alike had begun to grasp the changed situation. The New Far East was born.[31]

Japan's rapid industrialisation and modernisation fixed the standards and expectations. China not only lost the war with Japan, but the country also lost international respect and suffered from an increased negative global perception as Western explanations for China's rapid defeat centred around notions of a lack of both discipline and bravery in the army, widespread corruption, as well as a stubborn resistance to modernise institutions and practices.

At the beginning of hostilities, the press was already contemplating China's weaknesses. *The North-China Herald*, for example, brought attention to China's examination system, by asking,

> Who for instance but raving maniacs . . . would think of compelling all their mandarins and scholars to devote all their energies to the study of small ancient principalities . . . which are all dead thousands of years ago, while living nations which to-day singly possess more power than all those ancient ones put together are not worth a thought in their studies?[32]

Punch concurred with this assessment, explaining that the Government of China is "a vast system of competitive examination tempered by bribery." Students study "the works of CONFUCIUS, the history of China, and the art of writing as practised by the old masters" and if successful, they are "sent all over the country to be magistrates, generals, ship captains, engineers, without having the slightest acquaintance with details of systems over which they are put in a position of command."[33]

By the end of the war, reports explaining reasons for China's defeat were definitive. The front page of *The Pall Mall Gazette* declared that Chinese officers "possessed neither courage nor tactical knowledge" and whenever they could, "they ran away, and it was only when escape was impossible that they fought."[34] *The North-China Herald* remarked that "corruption [is] the main element in every part of the Chinese system" and that the word "Dishonesty" appears to "sum up the causes of China's fall."[35] *The Times* reported that a "more hopeless spectacle of fatuous imbecility, made up in equal parts of arrogance and helplessness, than the central Government of the Chinese Empire presented . . . is almost impossible to conceive."[36] By contrast Japan was praised for its rapid and successful modernisation programmes and technological achievements.[37] Western admiration was, however, short lived as concerns quickly developed over the threat of Japan as a formidable imperialist power. Sambourne captures Japan's new position in China in the Large Cut, "Jap in the China Shop" depicting a small Japanese man grabbing a rotund Chinese man by his queue (Figure 5.5).

The cartoon uses many of the visual tropes found in "Jap the Giant Killer" and "Little Ah Sid": the Chinese man is twice the size of the Japanese figure but proves to be no match. While there is a repetitive visual theme, Milliken's accompanying text presents something different for readers to consider. The Japanese man tells

THE JAP IN THE CHINA SHOP.

FIGURE 5.5 "The Jap in the China Shop" *Punch*, Vol. 108 (27 April 1895), p. 194.

Source: Punch, or The London Charivari

China to "Throw open your markets, and leave it to *Me*!" and to "Take down all your shutters, and hand *me* the key!" The text ends with Japan asking,

> Excuse me this wink, – but what do *you* think?
> Do you hold "Outside Devils" will suffer
> The Flowery Land to be locked by my hand,
> Any more than by yours, in their faces?[38]

Milliken points to an awareness that despite global recognition of Japan's rapid modernisation, Western powers will not respect the Japanese as equal players on the international arena. Commenting on the possibility of an Anglo-Japanese alliance, *The North-China Herald* declared that "Japan is, and must inevitably remain, an Oriental Power, and it has not as yet fallen to England's lot to play knife to any Asiatic Power's fork."[39] There is also a certain degree of anxiety in Milliken's text, as the Japanese figure is clearly intent on expanding his interests in China; Japan is therefore presented as a new and powerful imperial rival.

Punch was quick to understand this significance. As early as December 1894, Sambourne's Large Cut, "The Infant Phenomenon" represents Japan as a confident youngster lecturing on the art of war to a room full of Europeans (Figure 5.6). While the cartoon puts forward the idea that Japan, an Asian nation, could indeed be a world power, Milliken's accompanying text offers a

THE INFANT PHENOMENON.

FIGURE 5.6 "The Infant Phenomenon" *Punch*, Vol. 107 (22 December 1894), p. 290.

Source: Punch, or The London Charivari

word of caution: "If a kid, he's not a fool!" and ends with a warning that John Bull "Thinks the infant Jap a chap to keep *his* eye on!"[40] As admiration dispelled into anxiety in the wake of a victorious Japan, the daily news began reporting on the new global situation. *The Pall Mall Gazette* published a front-page article explaining that Britain must nowreckon with a new Power in the East, and a power which success may be expected to render aggressive. . . . We are manifestly the Power most affected, as we have colonies and commerce in every quarter of the earth.[41]

The Times stated that "Until little more than a twelvemonth ago Great Britain had enjoyed for upwards of 50 years . . . almost undisputed ascendancy in the Far East. . . . Within the following 12 months the situation was completely changed."[42]

The Sino-Japanese war had a devastating impact on China. It not only upset the traditional balance of power between China, Japan, and Korea, but it also highlighted the incompetence and weakness of the Qing court for the world to witness. To many, China's demise was considered imminent and therefore the partitioning of its territory was simply a matter of course. *The North-China Herald* reported that China "lost her prestige which was nothing but the shadow of a great name." It correctly predicts the scramble for concessions by declaring that China,

> Lies exposed as a carcass in the neighbourhood of which a cloud of eagles is hovering; that her independence is gone for the moment, and that on pain of permanent extinction as an autonomous Power she must submit to a prolonged tutelage; that if she does not honestly and unreservedly accept the position of a learner, from within, that position will be rudely forced on her from without.[43]

The post-war attitude towards China was contemptuous and imperial powers no longer hesitated in carving up spheres of influence among themselves. Indeed, the feeling was one of moral justification: if China was incapable of governing itself, then the powers *should* step in and take control over its corrupt institutions.[44] This led to a scramble for Chinese territory and the resulting imperial anxieties within a new geopolitical order gave *Punch* plenty of material to satirise.

The scramble for China

Picturing anxieties

In May 1898, Lord Salisbury gave his now famous and frequently quoted "dying nations" speech to the Primrose League. He predicted that "the living nations will gradually encroach on the territory of the dying and the seeds of conflict among civilized nations will gradually appear."[45] Salisbury could not have realised the accuracy of his perception. The result of the Sino-Japanese war not only placed China among "dying nations," but the war also exposed China's weakness at a time of new expansionist ideas among Great Power politics. Russia's interest in Manchuria and other outer provinces as well as its close proximity to China positioned Russia as an immediate threat to Britain. The Franco-Russian Alliance intended to check German power in Europe but was also directed against Britain. The transformation of geopolitical power directly affected Britain's global standing and Russia posed the most serious threat to British interests. China in the late nineteenth century thus became a site upon which imperial anxieties and power dynamics were both shaped and negotiated. It was during this time of heightened international tensions that *Punch* created Large Cuts reflecting Britain's evolving relationship with rival powers and used its cartoons to justify Britain's presence in China.

In Tenniel's "John Stands Aloof," a rotund Chinese man loses a game of cards and sits with his mouth hanging open in bewilderment as his Japanese opponent smiles and collects his winnings. Britain, Russia, Germany, and France watch the game and Russia is visibly unhappy (Figure 5.7). He stands directly over the game, points to the victorious Japanese man and furrows his eyebrows in disapproval. He asks John Bull, "Is he to have all this?" Standing off to the side, looking unconcerned while smoking a pipe, Britain answers "Well – he's played a square game – *I* don't see any call to interfere."[46] Milliken's accompanying text further clarifies Britain's stance,

> But the hands [Japan] has played
> With that Heathen Chinee,
> And the points he has made,
> Are, as far as I see,
> The result of good play *plus* good fortune;
> And *does* it concern you or me?
>
> The Russ standing by
> Turned his glance upon me.
> (For the JAP's pile *was* high.)
> And he hissed, "Shall this be?
> Must I have this smart JAP for a neighbour?
> Shall *he* clear out the Heathen Chinee?"
>
> Swarthy FRANÇOIS looked glum,
> Ginger HANS rubbed his chin:
> but I smoked and stood mum,
> As the JAP raked the tin.
> Then I says, "He's played fairly and squarely.
> So what call have *we* to cut in?[47]

The cartoon suggests that Britain had no need to concern itself over Japan emerging as a strong imperial force and that Japan's code of conduct in warfare was "played fairly and squarely." In reality, Japan could be a useful ally in challenging

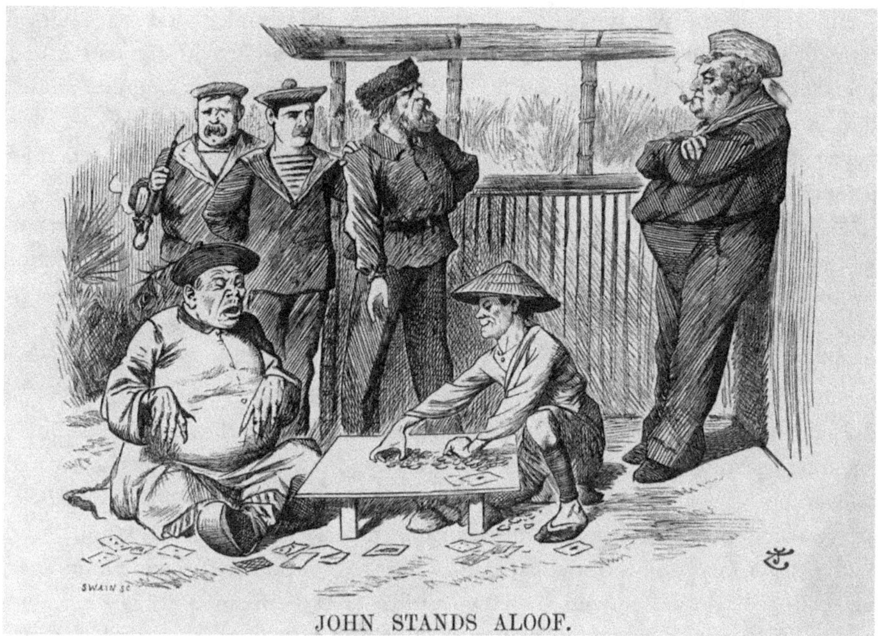

FIGURE 5.7 "John Stands Aloof" *Punch*, Vol. 108 (4 May 1895), p. 211.

Source: Punch, or The London Charivari

Russian expansion and thus it was in the interest of Britain that John Bull keep "mum."

The cartoon also points to Britain's isolation policy, which was coming under close scrutiny with the shift in international power that upset the political status quo in China. Britain was hyper sensitive to the terms of the Treaty of Shimonoseki, knowing there was a delicate balance between siding with China, in order to secure British interests, and siding with Japan, the new imperial power and potential future ally. The newly arrived British ambassador at St. Petersburg, Sir Frank Lascelles suggested "that it would be unwise to make an enemy of a Power which was obtaining a preponderant position in the Far East."[48] Britain therefore chose to "stand aloof" and held no firm policy; instead, Britain endeavoured to bring about a peace settlement, which would effectively maintain its dominant position. The decision to appear neutral had its consequences, as exemplified by the subsequent political manoeuvring between the powers to provide China with a substantial loan.

Britain declined participation in the Triple Intervention, even after several failed attempts from Russia, Germany, and France to enlist the British in applying pressure on Japan to give up its claim of the Liaodong Peninsula. When the Qing court requested £50 million to pay the war indemnity, the British, French, and German governments strategised on how to get hold of such an enormous sum. The significance of this was not lost among the powers who understood that political influence over the vanquished nation rested to a large extent with the nation best able to provide the necessary loan for China's immediate financial requirements.[49] Russia moved in and made a firm offer, securing the right to finance the Qing government by bringing attention to its active role in assisting China in retaining possession of this strategic area when Britain refused to help.[50]

In July 1895, *The Spectator* commented on the changed dynamics of power in China. "Russia" it states, "becomes the creditor of China" and thus "the guarantor becomes the protector of the guaranteed Power, and the beneficiary State has to seek direction and advice from its patron" thereby Russia successfully secured "a position of predominance in China."[51] Later that year in October, *The Times* published a report declaring that Russia "assumes a protectorate over China, and can only be intended to overset the existing balance of power in the East."[52] The Sino-Japanese war not only exposed China's weakness, but post-war events also created a heightened awareness of geopolitics and power among international rivals. Britain was strategic in allowing a future possible alliance with Japan but competition with Russia increased in intensity. Russia may have won the first indemnity loan but China would subsequently borrow from Britain, Germany, and France.[53] Tenniel's "Embarras de Richesse" depicts a Chinese man at the "Hotel de L'Europe" (Figure 5.8). He appears undecided on which table he would like to dine as both menus offer the same meal: a large loan served especially for China.

FIGURE 5.8 "Embarras de Richesse" *Punch*, Vol. 114 (5 February 1898), p. 55.

Source: Punch, or The London Charivari

FIGURE 5.9 "A Thin Disguise" *Punch*, Vol. 109 (2 November 1895), p. 206.

Source: Punch, or The London Charivari

British anxieties and suspicion over Russian ambitions in China steadily increased in the months after the Treaty of Shimonoseki was settled. Representations of Russia as a marauding bear dominated *Punch* cartoons and reflected mistrust and imperial competition. As early as 1895, Sambourne's "A Thin Disguise" (Figure 5.9) and Tenniel's "Seaside Lodgings" (Figure 5.10) the following year depict Russia as a sneaky bear with ulterior motives. In the first, the Russian bear

"SEASIDE LODGINGS."

FIGURE 5.10 "Seaside Lodgings" *Punch*, Vol. 111 (19 December 1896), p. 295.

Source: Punch, or The London Charivari

is dressed in Chinese clothing and clutches a secret treaty with "Port Arthur" written across, as he stealthily crosses into Manchuria. Tenniel's Russian bear is a not-so innocent tourist, actively seeking lodgings around Port Arthur. The cartoons not only correctly predicted Russian ambitions upon Port Arthur, which subsequently came into their possession, but they also grasped the significance of Russian hopes to build a Siberian railway across Manchuria and control the Bohai Sea [Gulf of

Pechihli], which directly threatened British political and commercial interests in northern China.[54]

In March 1898, *The Times* published proceedings from the Royal United Service Institution grappling with "The Chinese Question: How it may affect our Imperial interests." Russia, it was said, "thoroughly understood how to deal with an Asiatic Power, and made herself feared." It went on to describe Russia as the "protector of China in a peculiar sense – she protected for a price" and the "great object of Russian policy was to utilize China for the territorial expansion of Russia." The solution to curb Russian imperialist ambitions is "to induce China, by pressure if necessary to adopt reforms which would be of advantage to all the world including herself."[55] British diplomats and politicians were, however, scornful about the possibility of reforms in China. Contrary to Western belief, China's humiliating defeat in the Sino-Japanese war and the subsequent carving up of the country into various foreign spheres of influence led the Chinese to the realisation that reform was indeed needed and necessary for the country's survival.

In 1898, the Guangxu emperor, determined to reform China and make the country strong, issued sweeping decrees aimed at reforming the political and social systems. The changes proved to be too drastic for conservatives and the Empress Dowager Cixi, the real power behind the throne, promptly rounded up and

FIGURE 5.11 "Artful Dowager" *Punch*, Vol. 115 (8 October 1898), p. 158.

Source: Punch, or The London Charivari

executed reformers who did not manage to flee to safety. The Guangxu emperor was put under house arrest and the Empress Dowager took over the reigns of control thereby putting an end to Guangxu's ambitious plans to modernise China along Western lines. Sambourne's "The Artful Dowager" ridiculed the intrigues of the Qing court by depicting Cixi as the real power in China. In the Large Cut, the Empress Dowager is pulling the ear and threatening to punish the Guangxu emperor, represented as a mere boy, for his ideas on modernising the country (Figure 5.11).

Frustrated with China's weakness, Sir Nicholas Roderick O'Conor, former minister to China believed the country "had endless opportunities to harken to our advice but she preferred the hug of the bear & she must now take the consequences."[56] In August 1899, Sambourne depicted the Russian bear coming across a Japanese man wooing a Chinese woman (Figure 5.12). "Look here, I say!" says Russia, "If there's any hugging to be done, *I'll* do it." The cartoon represents the rivalry between Russia and Japan for gains in China; however, it is unique among the *Punch* series of imperial narratives related to China. Moving away from the tropes of dragons and rotund useless Mandarins, Sambourne feminises China by representing the country as a female object of affection by two male rivals' desire for influence and control. The feminisation of China was not a new concept; from the 1790s, China became female in British discourse in order for the country to embody particular traits such as weak, irrational, and whimsical. Britain, of course, claimed a masculine identity that

FIGURE 5.12 "Untitled" *Punch*, Vol. 117 (16 August 1899), p. 74.

Source: Punch, or The London Charivari

encompassed strength, rational, and honour.[57] Sambourne's depiction of two lecherous imperial rivals put forward the idea that China is weak and in need of protection, and who better qualified for the role of protector than the British?

Alarmed at Russian rivalry, British merchants warned that Russia would ensure the end of free trade in China by installing protectionist tariffs and other measures

FIGURE 5.13 "Honour à La Russe" *Punch*, Vol. 114 (7 May 1898), p. 211.

Source: Punch, or The London Charivari

to close their sphere of influence from British trade.[58] Russia was eventually successful in acquiring its long-desired Liaodong Peninsula with the ports of Dalian [Talienwan] and Port Arthur with the understanding that Dalian would be a free port. Britain remained suspicious and viewed Russia's agreement with distrust and as Russia looked next to Manchuria to expand, the *Spectator* commented that "[Britain] shall not be excluded from Manchuria, but only unable to get in."[59]

FIGURE 5.14 "Open At Last!" *Punch*, Vol. 117 (23 August 1899), p. 91.

Source: Punch, or The London Charivari

FIGURE 5.15 "Sentinels" *Punch*, Vol. 114 (16 April 1898), p. 175.

Source: Punch, or The London Charivari

In 1898, Tenniel's "Honour à La Russe" (Figure 5.13) depicts an aggrieved British Lion confronting the Russian Bear's broken promise to allow merchant ships. A year later, Tenniel created "Open At Last!" (Figure 5.14) to illustrate the Russian Bear allowing free trade, much to Britain's relief, although this did little to relieve tension or approach a rapprochement.

Tenniel's "Sentinels" (Figure 5.15) and "The Fight for the Foot-Plate" (Figure 5.16) and Sambourne's "The Open Mouth" (Figure 5.17) depict the power

THE FIGHT FOR THE FOOT-PLATE.

FIGURE 5.16 "The Fight for the Foot-Plate" *Punch*, Vol. 116 (15 March 1899), p. 127.

Source: Punch, or The London Charivari

struggle between Britain and Russia over territory as well as control over infrastructure while simultaneously portraying China's inability to defend itself. Germany was also causing concern. As a recently unified nation, Germany arrived late in the colonial game and had its own global aspirations. The murder of two German missionaries in 1897 in Shandong province was used as an opportunity to expand imperial ambitions and in March 1898, Germany leased the Bay of Jiaozhou [Kiaochow] with its harbour Qingdao [Tsingtao] on the coast of the Yellow Sea.[60] The German pretext to further its own imperial ambitions was not lost in China nor among the powers. In January 1898, The New York *Herald* published an interview with the famous Chinese statesman, Li Hongzhang, in which Li pointed out how the murder of German missionaries was used "just to oppress us." He added, "Should China be distressed by having her shores invaded and her territory occupied because of an occurrence which Western countries would deal with by law and not by war?"[61]

Sambourne's Large Cut, "A New Rôle," captures German ambitions. Kaiser Wilhelm is dressed in Chinese clothing, pulling up his moustache while admiring himself in a mirror (Figure 5.18). The caption has him thinking out loud, "Um-ha!" he muses, "With just a few additional touches here and there, I shall make a first-rate Emperor of China!"[62] *Punch* also brought attention to the German pretext

FIGURE 5.17 "The Open Mouth; or, the Integrity of China" *Punch*, Vol. 116 (10 May 1899), p. 218.

Source: Punch, or The London Charivari

to acquiring Chinese territory. "Compensation" provides a *quid pro quo* satirical list of German demands should any citizen fall into misfortune on Chinese soil:

To 1 Missionary, killed	200,000 taels.
Ditto	1 Cathedral, complete
Ditto ditto	50 square miles of territory.
To 1 Sailor, killed	1 Railway concession
1 Colonel, insulted	1,000 square miles of territory
2 Colonels, wounded	1 Province
1 General, killed	The Chinese Empire[63]

In Sambourne's "What Will They Do With 'Em?" the instability of friendship and co-operation between Germany and China is highlighted as the Kaiser and the Emperor of China comically battle with the other's national symbols (Figure 5.18).

With the full realisation of German imperial ambitions in China, Henry Bax-Ironside, the First Secretary at the Peking legation, predicted the Germans "will establish an 'imperium in imperio'" and apply "high-handed methods . . . in order to coerce the weak Government of Peking."[64] There was growing unease among the powers as rivals kept a watchful eye on each other and their interests in China.

FIGURE 5.18 “A New Rôle” *Punch*, Vol. 114 (15 January 1898), p. 14.

Source: Punch, or The London Charivari

FIGURE 5.19 "What Will They Do With 'Em?" *Punch*, Vol. 114 (18 June 1898), p. 278.

Source: Punch, or The London Charivari

Punch kept up-to-date with the latest proceedings and was quick to point out opportunistic activities by rival powers. Russia was consistently represented as a scheming and untrustworthy bear whereas Germany was depicted as a zealous imperialist. Remarking on the two imperial rivals, *Punch* quipped: "*Germany and Russia (to China).* Tea and turn out? No, thank you. We both prefer to take a little Chinese port, and consider that it will be all the better for keeping."[65]

An opportunity to counterbalance German and Russian gains in China arrived in the form of a lease of Weihaiwei, although the port was only symbolically important. Weihaiwei was too isolated to be of much use militarily and therefore the War Office and the Admiralty quickly resolved to abandon plans to fortify the place. However, its location in Shandong, the same coastal province as Jiaozhou Bay, meant that the presence of Britain in the area checked German proceedings. Equally significant, it served to mollify Russophobic sentiments at home by reasserting Britain's status as a power thereby appealing to British public opinion.[66] In a letter to the editor, P.H. Colomb wrote to *The Times* explaining that Weihaiwei held a "political, quite as much as, or even more than, a strategical genesis." He explains the Chinese port should be considered "a pistol at the head of the opposite shore, Port Arthur" as well as an important reminder to the Chinese people "that we were not going to suffer another nation to assume a foremost place in the councils of China which we had so

A GAME OF SPECULATION.

FIGURE 5.20 "A Game of Speculation" *Punch*, Vol. 114 (15 January 1898), p. 19.

Source: Punch, or The London Charivari

long occupied."[67] During his years as prime minister and foreign secretary, Lord Salisbury understood the necessity of appeasing the British public and wrote, " 'the public' will require territorial or cartographic consolation in China. It will not be useful, & it will be expensive but as a matter of course we shall have to do it."[68]

Punch also understood the importance of public opinion and although Britain was depicted as one of the imperial players in the game of partitioning China, the series of cartoons justified Britain by representing China as a nation in need of British leadership and stability. Influential politicians and members of government concurred. The *Spectator* declared that the Foreign Secretary George Curzon is "almost entirely without hope that China will do anything for herself, or will become anything but an object of grasping attack to foreign Powers, attack from which she must be protected, if at all, by an exertion of British strength."[69] In *Punch*, however, Britain was represented in a paradoxical position.

Tenniel's "A Game of Speculation," for example, depicts Britain sitting alongside rival powers in a poker-game for control over China (Figure 5.19). On the one hand, Britain is seen as actively participating in the division of China; on the other, Britain's actions is justified by claiming that its role protected China's interests as well as the continued maintenance of the global balance of power. Two further Tenniel cartoons depict Britain's conflicting position: "Giving Him a Lift" (Figure 5.20) represent a protective John Bull reassuring China that with Britain's

FIGURE 5.21 "Giving Him a Lift" *Punch*, Vol. 114 (12 March 1898), p. 115.

Source: Punch, or The London Charivari

assistance, other imperial powers would not be able to easily take advantage of its weakened state. "Hold On, John!" (Figure 5.21) depicts the tug-of-war between European powers as they fight over control for Chinese territory and infrastructure.

The series of cartoons in *Punch* depicting the scramble for Chinese concessions did more than simply reflect imperial rivalries. The magazine used its cartoons to persuade readers that Britain's presence in China was justified by a repetitive representation of Russia as a sneaky bear and Germany as an ambitious and opportunistic imperialist. The narrative consistently promoted the idea that Britain's role was vital in order to maintain the balance of world power and ensure fair treatment for the Chinese against rivals with ulterior and questionable motives. China was further destabilised and the division of its territories gave rise to a violent backlash with the Boxer Uprising in early 1900, which would take the international community by surprise and place Japan as an ally alongside Western powers.

The Boxer Uprising

Cartooning tensions in the Eight-Nation Alliance

By the closing years of the nineteenth century, strong anti-foreign, anti-Christian sentiments permeated through China's social fabric and this was further aggravated by economic impoverishment, natural calamities, and growing Chinese nationalism. This combination provided the foundation for a violent demonstration, known as the Boxer Uprising, against Chinese and foreign Christians as well as the foreign community in China. The Boxers were composed mainly of Chinese peasants, made desperate after a series of famines and droughts in the Shandong area. They banded together to revolt against the increased expansion of Christianity into proper China and their aim was to support the Qing in eliminating foreigners and their religion from the country.[70]

Joseph W. Esherick notes that the Shandong area where the Boxers originated was largely composed of Catholics and thus it was the Catholics rather than other Christian denominations that resentment and anger were directed towards. As Esherick explains, although the "Protestant converts would soon find themselves caught up in the growing anti-Christian movement, the primary Boxer animus was directed at the Catholics." Chinese Christians were also targets. They were, much like the foreigners in China, disliked and distrusted because many converted for opportunistic reasons and used their connection with foreign priests and churches to gain benefits. Admiral Tirpitz, secretary of state of the German Naval Ministry and chief architect of Germany's naval development, wrote to the Jiaozhou governor regarding events in 1899. He believed that "the uproar in Shantung was caused by the Catholic missionaries in general, and the provocative behavior of the Chinese Christians in particular."[71]

With tensions and animosity simmering, the Boxers targeted railroads, telegraph systems, and missionaries, all of which were, from a Western perspective, important

FIGURE 5.22 "Hold On, John!" *Punch*, Vol. 114 (2 April 1898), p. 151.

Source: Punch, or The London Charivari

FIGURE 5.23 "The Same Old Bear" *Punch*, Vol. 118 (13 June 1900), p. 419.

Source: Punch, or The London Charivari

FIGURE 5.24 "A Legacy of Discord" *Punch*, Vol. 118 (27 June 1900), p. 459.

Source: Punch, or The London Charivari

FIGURE 5.25 "Rubbing It In!" *Punch*, Vol. 119 (4 July 1900), p. 11.

Source: Punch, or The London Charivari

symbols of progress and modernity and for these reasons, Western representations framed the event in a simplistic dichotomy of "civilisation" against "barbarism" and "backwardness." The Qing Court was aware of the uprising but did nothing as it was divided between pro- and anti-Boxer factions and with its inaction, the violence increased. Western news media started to make note of the Boxers in the autumn of 1899 and in early June 1900, several Europeans were killed and a larger group of Boxers began activities in and around Beijing and Tianjin. Media reports, visual documentation, and witness accounts, along with fictionalised adventure stories for children, and stage productions[72] sensationalised the event, in particular the siege of the Beijing legation, which replaced the Anglo-Boer War as headline news in British papers.[73]

In America, a stage production of the siege of the foreign community in the Beijing legation was a tremendous success. In April of 1901, the dramatic theatre production, *The Rescue at Pekin*, was met with popular enthusiasm and patriotic zeal. John R. Haddad asserts that the performance was intended to be "an elaborate spectacle that would stir the hearts of spectators with patriotism, awe them with its gigantism, and overload their senses with its colourful pageantry, thrilling action, incessant gun firing, and booming pyrotechnical explosions." *The Rescue at Pekin* proved so successful that the attendance "often exceeded the populations of the host cities" as people came in from nearby towns and the countryside. The Boxers

FIGURE 5.26 "To Pekin!" *Punch*, Vol. 119 (18 July 1900), p. 47.

Source: Punch, or The London Charivari

were also portrayed in American films such as *Tortured by Boxers* (1900) and *Rescue of a White Girl from the Boxers* (1900).[74]

The international interest and excitement surrounding the Boxer Uprising marked yet another significant turning point in China's relationship with the global community as the discourse on Chinese people proliferated the idea of a menacing and threatening people with intense hatred towards foreigners. By the middle of the month, the international legations issued a call for help to the coast and the foreign community took refuge in the Legation Quarter. Empress Dowager Cixi finally decided to support the uprising against the foreigners and on 20 June, the Qing regiment and Boxers combined forces and laid siege to the legation, which lasted until 14 August.[75]

As a response, an international military coalition was formed; the eight nations were Britain, Japan, Russia, France, America, Germany, Italy, and Austria-Hungary. They were called the Eight-Nation Alliance and numbered 20,000 personnel, half of whom were Japanese troops.[76] This was essentially an international mandate for Japan to lead in the relief of the legation in the hopes of counterbalancing Russian predominance. Salisbury held an interview with the Japanese diplomatic representative, pressing upon him "the fact that the opportunity was now theirs; if they did not intervene effectively disorder might increase, & if there was a general break-up, Russia would dominate Pekin which ought not suit their views."[77]

FIGURE 5.27 "Quite at Home" *Punch*, Vol. 120 (20 March 1901), p. 223.

Source: Punch, or The London Charivari

Britain remained deeply suspicious of Russian designs on China's northern territory and anxious that Russia would establish itself at Beijing [Peking] after the uprising was quelled. *Punch*'s caption in "The Same Old Bear" reveals the deep mistrust between the two nations: "You've got so much to do elsewhere, *I'll* tackle this obstreperous party" says the Russian Bear to the British Lion (Figure 5.22). "Oh, thanks! But I wouldn't leave you alone with him for worlds!" replies Britain.

Navigating international rivalries amidst deep distrust while simultaneously joining forces for a common cause was complex and precarious. Tenniel's "A Legacy of Discord," captures anxieties that stemmed from competition with other imperial rivals over power and control in East Asia, and not from dealing with China, a nation that posed no lasting or significant threat to British interests. Tenniel's cartoon depicts a lone Chinese soldier facing the coalition and tells them, "You allee chop-chop me now, but welly soon forrin devil chop-chop forrin devil!" (Figure 5.23).

Japan also featured in the cartoons as the new imperial rival. Tenniel's "Rubbing It In!" depicts a fully armed Japanese soldier addressing the coalition, "Delighted to join you, gentlemen; but permit me to remark that if some of you hadn't interfered when *I* had him down, it would have saved all this trouble!" (Figure 5.24). The treatment Japan received in 1895 resulted in Japan's suspicions of the powers and their intentions. There were five occasions when Britain and Russia attempted to intervene during the First Sino-Japanese war to quickly end the conflict and Japan was reluctant to do so as its forces were in a stronger position.[78] Then there was the pressure for the Japanese to retrocede the Liaodong Peninsula, which only deepened Japan's mistrust. "To Pekin!" captures this tension. "En Avant!" an eager Japanese soldier cries to his less-than-enthusiastic looking Russian ally who mutters, "I *do* hope his motives are as disinterested as mine" (Figure 5.25).

Despite deep distrust, once the Alliance was formed, it won a succession of victories against the poorly led imperial army. In August 1900, the international coalition reached Beijing and by this time, most Boxers discarded their weapons and dressed as ordinary citizens then quietly disappeared into the population. Cixi, the Emperor, and high court officials fled under armssed escort to Xi'an.[79] With victory for the Eight-Nation Alliance imminent, a punitive expedition was sent forth in Boxer strongholds around Tianjin and north and south of the capital. The German Field Marshal Alfred von Waldersee took command and launched a brutal expedition; much of Tianjin was destroyed, many villages were left in devastation, thousands of Chinese soldiers and civilians were killed and looting and plunder was endemic. The American photographer James Ricalton witnessed events. In Tianjin, he wrote, "Shamefully looted China has had a lesson in the ethics of Christian armies she will not soon forget."[80]

The mission was to avenge the murder of the German minister Baron Clemens von Ketteler, who was killed on his way to discuss matters with the Zongli Yamen before fighting began. More significantly, von Ketteler's death was employed as a means of advancing German interests in China, in much the same way as the Juye Incident a few years earlier.[81] Sambourne's "East and West," brings attention to Germany's imperial ambitions (see Chapter 2, Figure 2.6). Kaiser Wilhelm stands imperiously over the Chinese Emperor, on his knees with hands wringing in distress. He begs Germany, "I will make the expiations that Heaven demands!" to which Kaiser replies, "*And* – you will also make the *reparation* that I demand!" *Punch* tells its readers: if Germany is left unchecked, this overly ambitious, dictatorial nation will expand its interests by whatever means possible.[82] In another Large Cut, Sambourne's "Quite At Home" illustrates a fully armed Russian Cossack making himself comfortable in Manchuria (Figure 5.27). The cartoon references the distrust British politicians felt as Russia repeatedly tried to gain control over the British-run Imperial Maritime Customs Service and planned to invade Manchuria.[83]

The series that *Punch* created during the Boxer Uprising persuaded readers that the real threat to British interests in China were imperial rivals. While the Boxers came to exemplify China as a barbaric and primitive country waiting, indeed needing, to be redeemed by Christianity, *Punch* focused its attention primarily on the continued distrust and trepidation between rival powers, even with the apparent co-operation of the Eight-Nation Alliance. Russia and Germany were depicted as untrustworthy nations with questionable objectives while Japan emerged as an equal imperial player and represented as a formidable force. China's weakened position was consistently highlighted and was not a threat but became an important space upon which imperial rivalries were played out. The series of visual and textual satire that *Punch* created were used as a powerful tool to persuade readers that Britain's presence in China was both justified and a requirement in order to maintain the global balance of power.

Notes

1 "A Legacy of Discord" *Punch*, Vol. 118 (27 June 1900), p. 459.

2 "A Touching Appeal" *Punch*, Vol. 107 (17 November 1894), p. 234.

3 Miles Taylor, "John Bull and the Iconography of Public Opinion in England c. 1712–1929" *Past & Present*, No. 134 (February 1992), p. 100.

4 The language of pidgin was created to facilitate business between Chinese merchants and European traders along the southern coast of China and the word "pidgin" reflects its historical roots. From the lucrative trade, the language then spread to households where Chinese servants used this invaluable tool to communicate with their British employers. One gets a sense of how pidgin was used in a British household by Chinese servants in Martin Booth's memoir of his childhood spent in Hong Kong. Pidgin proved so useful a tool that Chinese phrase books were published in order to teach the Chinese this contact language, such as *The Language of the Red-haired Foreigners* that appeared around the beginning of the nineteenth century and *The Chinese-English Instructor* that was published around 1862 by a missionary school educated graduate named Tong Kit. Dr. Stephen Matthews, personal notes taken at the University of Hong Kong, 19 December 2016; Martin Booth, *Gweilo* (London: Bantham Books, 2005); Michelle Li, Stephen Matthews and Geoff P. Smith, "Pidgin English Texts from the Chinese English Instructor" *Chinese Pidgin English: Texts and Contexts* (eds.) Geoff P. Smith and Stephen Matthews, The English Centre; The University of Hong Kong, Vol. 10, No. 1 (September 2005), pp. 79–81; Zhang Zhenjian, *Language and Society in Early Hong Kong, 1841–1884*, unpublished Ph.D. Dissertation (University of Hong Kong), p. 182. Zhang explains that *The Chinese-English Instructor* "was very popular and rapidly made [Tong Kit] known nationally." p. 183.

5 Holger Kersten, "America's Multilingualism and the Problem of the Literary Representation of 'Pidgin English'" *Amerikastudien/American Studies*, Vol. 51, No. 1, Multilingualism and American Studies (2006), p. 78.

6 Li, Matthews, and Smith, "Pidgin English Texts from the Chinese English Instructor," p. 80.

7 Hoffman Atkinson, *Exercises in the Yokohama Dialect* (Yokohama: The Japan Gazette Office; 1879); Leland Charles Godfrey, "A New Dialect; or, Yokohama Pidgin" *New Quarterly Magazine*, London Vol. 2, (July 1879), pp. 114–124.

8 Altick, *Punch*, pp. 82–83.

9 Kersten, "America's Multilingualism," p. 76.

10 Hart to Campbell, 27 July 1894, The I.G. in Peking, Vol. 2, 979, as quoted in S. C. M. Paine, *The Sino-Japanese War of 1894–1895* (Cambridge; New York: Cambridge University Press, 2003), p. 127.

11 The Empress Dowager Cixi infamously depleted the naval funds since 1889 to renovate the Summer Palace for her sixtieth birthday celebrations
12 The Chinese army lacked much-needed ammunition and during open hostilities, found themselves with no shells for their Krupp canons and no gunpowder to load their Armstrong guns. After the 1894 Battle of the Yalu River, Japanese troops found that some of the Chinese shells were filled with cement or porcelain instead of explosives. See Bickers, *The Scramble for China*, p. 325; Paine, *The Sino-Japanese War,* pp. 181–182.
13 Paine, *The Sino-Japanese War,* p. 127.
14 Hart to Campbell, 8 July 1894, The I.G. in Peking, no. 933 as quoted in Bickers, *The Scramble for China,* p. 325; Paine states that "In Europe, numbers were still believed to be decisive: China was big, therefore it would win." *The Sino-Japanese War,* p. 156.
15 Paine, *The Sino-Japanese War,* p. 129.
16 "The Chino-Japanese War: The Art of Lying as Practiced in the East" *The Pall Mall Gazette,* (London, England), No. 9210 (29 September 1894), British Library Newspapers, p. 7.
17 "The Chino-Japanese War: Why the War News is Inaccurate" *The Pall Mall Gazette,* (London, England), No. 9219, Wednesday (10 October 1894), British Library Newspapers, p. 7.
18 "On the War in the East" *Punch,* Vol. 107 (22 September 1894), p. 133.
19 "Toning It Down" *Punch,* Vol. 108 (23 February 1895), p. 85.
20 Paine, *The Sino-Japanese War,* p. 189.
21 Paine, *The Sino-Japanese War,* p. 100; Judith Frohlich, "Pictures of the Sino-Japanese War of 1894–1895" *War in History,* Vol. 21, No. 2 (2014), pp. 215, 249; John W. Dower, "Throwing off Asia II: Symbolic 'China'" *MIT Visualising Cultures.* Online: http//ocw.mit.edu. Paine, *The Sino-Japanese War,* p. 100.
22 At the beginning of hostilities, the Japanese were criticised for its failure to save drowning Chinese soldiers after they torpedoing the British-owned but Chinese-leased vessel the *S.S. Kowshing.* The Japanese made an effort to rescue the Europeans but offered little help to the Chinese and of the 1,176 people on-board, only 205 survived. The British public reacted with outrage and the subsequent criticism upset the Japanese government. They changed tactics; instead, they used Chinese prisoners of war to highlight Japan's progress in the field of medicine as well as an ideal treatment of the captured and wounded Chinese soldiers. Howland points out that some argue that Japan attacked the *S.S. Kowshing* prior to their being open hostilities between China and Japan. For more, see Douglas Howland, "The Sinking of the S.S. Kowshing: International Law, Diplomacy, and the Sino-Japanese War" in *Modern Asian Studies,* Vol. 42, No. 4 (July 2008), pp. 673–703. Paine states that while there are numerous reports of the faultless care of prisoners captured at P'yôngyang, it is unclear whether other prisoners of war received the same treatment. Paine asserts that "diaries of Japanese soldiers suggest that Japanese forces were not interested in taking prisoners of war" and that "the Chinese were most frequently found shot or wounded in the back, as a rule without weapons, often only half clothed, as if they had torn their uniforms off in order to be mistaken for non-combatant Chinese." See Paine, *The Sino-Japanese War,* pp. 175–176.
23 "The Atrocities After the Fall of Port Arthur" *The Times* (8 January 1895), p. 6; "The Port Arthur Atrocities" *The Times* (1 February 1895), p. 4.
24 James Allan, *Under the Dragon Flag: My Experiences in the Chino-Japanese War* (London: W. Heinemann, 1898), p. 66.
25 Frederick Villiers "The Truth About Port Arthur" *The North American Review,* Vol. 160, No. 460 (March 1895), pp. 327–328.
26 "A Gentle Hint to the Jubilant Jap" *Punch,* Vol. 108 (19 January 1895), p. 35.
27 Front Coverart, *Punch,* Vol. 107 (11 August 1894), n.p.
28 "Jap the Giant-Killer" *Punch,* Vol. 107 (29 September 1894), p. 150.
29 "The War in the East" *The Times* (26 December 1894), p. 4, cited in Paine, *The Sino-Japanese War,* p. 237.
30 Linley Sambourne Diary, Saturday October 13, 1894.
31 Arthur Diósy, "The New Japan" *Japan as Seen and Described by Famous Writers,* edited and translated by Esther Singleton (New York: Dodd Mead and Co., 1904), p. 363.

32 "The Disease of China" *The North-China Herald* (Shanghai), (10 August 1894), p. 219.
33 "Our Booking Office" *Punch*, Vol. 108 (6 April 1895), p. 165.
34 "The Lessons of the Naval War in the East" *The Pall Mall Gazette*, 4th Edition, (22 February 1895), front page.
35 "The Problem of China's Fall" *The North-China Herald* (Shanghai), (5 April 1895), p. 504.
36 "The Far Eastern Question" *The Times*, (26 September 1895), p. 6.
37 Paine notes that Field-Marshal Yamagata was receiving so many daily congratulatory letters (mostly from Britain and America) on the success of the war that he needed to hire half a dozen translators to handle the amount of correspondence. *The Sino-Japanese War*, pp. 292–293.
38 "Jap in the China Shop" *Punch*, Vol. 108 (27 April 1895), p. 195.
39 "An Anglo-Japanese Alliance" *The North-China Herald* (Shanghai), (3 May 1895), p. 646.
40 "The Infant Phenomenon" *Punch*, Vol. 107 (22 December 1894), p. 291.
41 "The Lessons of the Naval War in the East" *The Pall Mall Gazette* (London), (2 February 1895), pp. 1–2. Cited in Paine, *The Sino-Japanese War*, p. 301.
42 "England's Position Before and After the War," *The Times*, (24 September 1895), p. 3.
43 "The Problem of China's Fall" *The North-China Herald* (Shanghai), (5 April 1895), p. 504.
44 Paine, *The Sino-Japanese War*, p. 304.
45 Cited in T. G. Otte, *The China Question: Great Power Rivalry and British Isolation, 1894–1905* (New York: Oxford University Press, 2007), p. 2.
46 "John Stands Aloof" *Punch*, Vol. 108 (4 May 1895), p. 211.
47 "John Stands Aloof" *Punch*, Vol. 108 (4 May 1895), pp. 210–211.
48 Cited in Otte, *The China Question*, p. 57.
49 D. McLean, "The Foreign Office and the First Chinese Indemnity Loan, 1895" *The Historical Journal*, Vol. 16, No. 2 (June 1973), p. 303.
50 Russia was the first to react by quickly mobilising the Triple Intervention to forestall Japan's possession of the strategic Liaodong Peninsula in southern Manchuria. With the support of France and Germany, Russia was able to persuade the Japanese to retrocede the Liaodong Peninsula in return for a larger indemnity. Japan was furious but understood the limitations of their military. It may have been able to beat China but it would not have the same success if confronted with a united foreign military. The Japanese accepted the terms resentfully and came to comprehend the reality of global politics; viz. they were not respected or treated as an equal with Western powers. Japan learned that only by strengthening its military and becoming a true formidable rival, could they protect their national interests. Charles Nelson Spinks, "The Background of the Anglo-Japanese Alliance" *Pacific Historical Review*, Vol. 8, No. 3 (September 1939), p. 320; for the complexities in Britain's decision to remain neutral, see D. McLean, "The Foreign Office and the First Chinese Indemnity Loan, 1895," pp. 303–321; Otte, *The China Question*, Chapter 1, pp. 28–73.
51 "Russia's Policy in the Far East" *The Spectator* (13 July 1895), p. 37.
52 "Russia and China" *The Times* (28 October 1895), p. 5.
53 Dower, "Throwing off Asia III: Spoils of War." Online: http//ocw.mit.edu.
54 McLean, "The Foreign Office and the First Chinese Indemnity Loan, 1895," p. 316.
55 "The British Aspect of the Chinese Question" *The Times* (10 March 1898), p. 12.
56 O'Conor cited in Otte, *The China Question*, p. 112.
57 Hevia, *Cherishing Men from Afar*, pp. 73–74.
58 Kees van Dijk, *Pacific Strife: The Great Powers and Their Political and Economic Rivalries in Asia and the Western Pacific 1870–1914* (Amsterdam: Amsterdam University Press, 2015), p. 36.
59 Cited in *The North China Herald*, "Russia Shows Her Hand" (14 March 1898), p. 404.
60 The incident is known as the Juye Incident and refers to the night of All Saints' Day when two German Catholic missionaries belonging to the Society of the Divine Word, Richard Henle and Francis Xavier Nies, were murdered during their visit and stay with a third member of the Order, Georg M. Stenz. Stenz was stationed in the area, in Juye County, Shandong Province, and he was known as an "unusually offensive individual," interfering in Chinese lawsuits,

punishing those who were perceived to insult the church, and accused of more than ten rapes of local women. By chance and a curious twist of fate, he was the only survivor although he was most likely the intended target for he aroused acrimony among the population. Although others suggest that it was Henle who was the target of the attack as he was difficult and unpopular. Writing about the incident in the introduction to his book *Life of Father Richard Henle, S.V.D.*, Stenz states that as a consequence to the murders, "The Chinese Government agreed upon the conditions made by the German Government – the deposition of certain officers, known as Christian-haters, and the erection of three expiation churches." Indeed, the Qing transferred or dismissed some local officials as well as removed Li Bingheng, the Shandong governor, who appeared to have had nothing to do with the incident, and cathedrals were built at the expense of the Chinese governments. See Georg Maria Stenz, *Life of Father Richard Henle, S.V.D.: Missionary in China: Assassinated November 1, 1897* (Techny, IL: Mission Press, S.V.D., 1915); Joseph Esherick, *The Origins of the Boxer Uprising* (Berkeley; London: University of California Press, 1987), pp. 125–126; Paul A. Cohen, *History in Three Keys: The Boxers as Event, Experience, and Myth* (New York: Columbia University Press, 1997), pp. 20–21.

61 Cited in "The Situation in the Far East" *The Times* (4 January 1898), p. 3.

62 "A New Rôle" *Punch*, Vol. 114 (15 January 1898), p. 14.

63 "Compensation" *Punch*, Vol. 114 (12 February 1898), p. 69.

64 Cited in Otte, *The China Question*, p. 113.

65 Untitled, *Punch*, Vol. 114 (8 January 1898), p. 5.

66 Otte, *The China Question*, pp. 130–131.

67 "Wei-Hai-Wei" *The Times* (26 May 1899), p. 3.

68 Salisbury to Chamberlain, 30 December 1897, Chamberlain MSS, Birmingham University Library, JC 5/67/88. Cited in T. G. Otte, "'Avenge England's Dishonour': By-Elections, Parliament and the Politics of Foreign Policy in 1898" *The English Historical Review*, Vol. 121, No. 491 (April 2006), p. 389.

69 "News of the Week" *The Spectator* (5 March 1898), p. 326.

70 Esherick, *The Origins of the Boxer Uprising*, p. 253.

71 Esherick, *The Origins of the Boxer Uprising*, for Catholics being the original primary target, see p. 242. For Admiral Tirpitz, see pp. 204–205.

72 Ross. G. Forman, "Peking Plots: Fictionalizing the Boxer Rebellion of 1900" in *Victorian Literature and Culture*, Vol. 27, No. 1 (1999), p. 20, footnote 16.

73 Forman, "Peking Plots," p. 23; Otte, *The China Question*, p. 181.

74 John R. Haddad, "The Wild West Turns East: Audience, Ritual, and Regeneration in Buffalo Bill's Uprising" *American Studies*, Vol. 49, No. 3/4 (Fall/Winter 2008), *Rescue of Pekin*, p. 18; discussion of films, p. 26.

75 Hevia, *English Lessons*, pp. 191–192.

76 Cohen, *History in Three Keys*, pp. 52–54. The Eight-Nation Alliance consisted of Britain, Germany, France, Russia, America, Japan, Austria, and Italy.

77 Cited in Otte, *The China Question*, p. 187.

78 Ian Nish, "Politics, Trade and Communications in East Asia: Thoughts on Anglo-Russian Relations, 1861–1907" *Modern Asian Studies*, Vol. 21, No. 4 (1987), p. 673.

79 Cohen, *History in Three Keys*, p. 54; Esherick, *The Origins of the Boxer Uprising*, p. 310.

80 James Ricalton, *China Through the Stereoscope; a Journey Through the Dragon Empire at the Time of the Boxer Uprising* (New York: Underwood & Underwood, 1901), p. 233.

81 Cohen, *History in Three Keys*, p. 55.

82 I am referring specifically *Punch* cartoons of Kaiser Wilhelm in relation to China. Richard Scully notes that representations of Wilhelm in *Punch* have been highly selected to reveal a negative perspective before World War I; however, Scully argues that the cartoons were much more multifaceted and when considering the series, rather than selection, of images, there were just as many positive representations of the Kaiser. See Scully, "A Pettish Little Emperor." Online: http://books.publishing.monash.edu.

83 Forman, "Peking Plots," p. 21.

6

CONCLUSION

In *Punch's Almanack for 1901*, Sir Bernard Partridge depicts the nations of the world gambling. At the front of the image, a despondent-looking Chinese man is playing a game of roulette with Father Time. The wheel, labelled "Twentieth Century," is next to the sands of time, a visual metaphor for the inevitability of change and of mortality. The Chinese man is lost in thought as he sits among the world but is disengaged from the other players. Father Time is the only figure that takes an interest in this melancholy player; as the croupier, he is dealing out China's fate for the twentieth century. Is the cartoon's message telling us that it is only a matter of time before China loses the global game of imperialism? Or is it saying that only time will tell how things will play out in China? Partridge's prediction for China's future did not appear optimistic. The beginning of the twentieth century opened with the signing of the Boxer Protocol that officially ended the Boxer Uprising and placed China at the forefront of British public consciousness.

More than any other event in China, the Uprising attracted the attention of news media around the world and the visual and textual narratives gave rise to a fixed set of stereotypes and myths of the Chinese that would have lasting impressions on the Western imagination. In November 1900, *Punch* published a contribution from a Mr. Fox Russell, satirising a diary entry from a "Mandarin Lo-Fun" where "Lo-Fun" writes, "Foreign devils still pressing for punishment of high officials. Sent for HANG-HI-CHOP" to send the foreign powers the "heads of four or five brace of coolie prisoners."[1] The irony of this entry lies in the Chinese demands of execution when in reality, one of the demands by foreign powers to settle for peace was the death of pro-Boxer officials in the form of execution or by suicide, with the exception of Prince Duan who was allowed lifetime exile in Xinjiang.[2] This "diary" entry, while it acknowledges foreign demands to punish those involved in supporting the Boxers, it ignores the death sentence required by the foreign powers. Instead, it turns the tables on the Chinese, making it appear that it is "them" and not "us" who are ruled by despotic "off-with-your-head" officials.

DOI: 10.4324/9781003025573-6

FIGURE 6.1 "Make Your Game!" *Punch Almanack for 1901*, n.p.

Source: Punch, or The London Charivari

Chinese corporal punishment became a Western fascination and public executions were photographed by foreigners and circulated abroad for publication in various newspapers, journals, and books. The images were also turned into postcards, sent along with personal letters to friends and family, or collected for personal use. The popularity of these photographs not only revealed the interest

FIGURE 6.2 "Outside, Sir! Outside!" *Punch*, Vol. 94 (2 June 1888), p. 255.

Source: Punch, or The London Charivari

and demand for such "Chinese" sights but they also formed an important part of constructing the idea that there was an irreconcilable difference between the East and the West.[3] James Hevia asserts that the events surrounding the Boxers signified "deep-seated Western anxieties about global cross-cultural relations" and China became both an example and a symbol of incompatibility and divide between the East and the West. Cruelty and violence was promulgated as "what the Eastern half of that dichotomy looked like."[4] After the Boxer events, China was held in even lower esteem worldwide.[5]

Unbeknownst to Partridge, he was correct in depicting a forlorn and dispirited Chinese man in *Punch*'s *Almanack for 1901*. The twentieth century gave rise to a

"Yellow Peril" discourse that coincided with the global downward spiral of negative perceptions of China and Chinese people. It was Kaiser Wilhelm II who, in 1895, popularised the phrase, "Yellow Peril" during the First Sino-Japanese war when he sent his cousin, Tsar Nicholas II, an allegorical lithograph by the artist Hermann Knackfuss. The lithograph depicts the people of Europe, led by Germany and Christianity, in their fight against the invasion of the people of the East. The outline of the Buddha is shown in the background, surrounded by menacing dark clouds and lightning, or, by some interpretations, by the smoke of a burning village. The caption reads "Peoples of Europe, Guard Your Most Sacred Possessions."[6]

The "Yellow Peril" discourse demonised the Chinese as opium addicts and sex deviants. The consistent and repetitive tropes pointed to anxieties of a menacing China outnumbering and enslaving Western people as well as reflected a fear of economic competition by Chinese labourers working on Western soil and cultural degeneracy through contact with the Chinese.[7] The "Yellow Peril" discourse was significant in shaping the way the Chinese were perceived worldwide and these anxieties and xenophobic sentiments affected politics and policies in restricting immigration. Sambourne's June 1888 allegorical figure of Australia refers to the Australian Intercolonial Conference on the Chinese Question further restricting Chinese immigration (Figure 6.2). The cartoon exemplifies fears of a rising and powerful East, bent on invasion and conquering the "White" race.[8] In 1877, Sir Archibald Michie, the former Attorney-General of Victoria, declared Chinese immigration into Australia was problematic because the "two people can never amalgamate."[9]

Britain shared these concerns. The negligible Chinese community became an ideal foil for a variety of grievances in British society from struggling workers to gender relations and the supposed incompatibility between the Chinese and Anglo-Saxons dominated British discourse in the early twentieth century.[10] The trope of barbaric, evil Chinese became standard in a variety of visual genres. W.J.T. Mitchell describes stereotypes as "a virus that resists all efforts at eradication or immunization" and adds that if any images take on "a 'life of its own,' it would seem to be the racial stereotype."[11] By converting popular images from caricatures to theatre and eventually films and into the daily press and popular novels, "representations of the Chinese underscored the implication that there was nothing to choose between the two."[12] Edward Said recognised the significance of this repetitive tendency to homogenise the discourse. He commented on viewers watching films about "Crusades, *Arabian Nights* films, Imperial films, films with exotic Chinese – all of them are very difficult to remove from our head when later on you grow up and you *read the books*."[13]

Punch's visual and textual satire played an important part of this narrative by constructing a fixed idea of China and the Chinese in the British popular imagination. The series coincided and reinforced a homogenised narrative thereby translating *Punch*'s discourse from entertainment into something much more serious. The magazine's widespread circulation of "knowledge" was a significant part of an important network of information dissemination and functioned as a vehicle that shaped perceptions of the self and "other." It would be useful to have evidence about effects, readers' responses, and the ways in which the cartoons directly translated into treatment of the Chinese community living in Britain. However, evidence is fragmented; in the words of L. Perry Curtis, Jr., the creation of these images arise from "prejudices [that] can be traced directly from the cartoons back to that vast subterranean culture – unwritten and full of slang – which has no place in our respectable history books."[14]

During the course of this research, I have been unable to find the voice of an "everyday" Chinese person during the Victorian era in order to get a sense of the ways in which these images translated into treatment of the Chinese community living in Britain. Sun Yat-sen wrote about his experiences being detained at the Chinese Legation in London in 1896 but he said little about his daily life, focusing instead on his kidnapping and detention to garner support against the Chinese government. Lao She's fictional novel *Mr. Ma and Son* offers more insight into how the Chinese were treated in London. However, he was writing at a time when anti-Chinese sentiments were at its height. Gregor Benton and Edmund Terence Gomez note that antipathy towards the Chinese was at its peak around the turn of the century and thus Lao She's experience of living in London in the 1920s may have differed from the Chinese experience in the 1850s.[15]

There were, and continue to be, no singular, static representation of the Chinese. *Punch*'s series of cartoons from 1841 to 1901 demonstrate that while the trope of imagery of the Chinese generally remained consistent and repetitive, the message in the cartoons offer a changing and shifting trajectory that coincided with developing Sino-British relations. *Punch*'s textual and visual satires provide a fascinating glimpse into the magazine's perspective on Britain's position among the global community and a textured lens into wider anxieties about the state of foreign relations vis-à-vis the British social class system as well as Britain's self-perception as an imperial power.

Why study political cartoons? Indeed, how relevant are cartoons and caricatures for modern audiences? The satirical magazine *Private Eye* celebrated its 50th anniversary in 2011 selling an average of almost 230,000 copies a fortnight with sales figures rising 10.1% over the previous year.[16] The newspaper *Independent* published a commentary in 2017 stating, "as newspaper circulation continues to founder, sales of satire and current affairs magazines have never looked healthier" and notes that *Private Eye*'s "circulation soars as readers turn to satire."[17] The continued popularity of this form of visual means that they deserve careful consideration and we could only benefit in understanding their power and influence in society. Without critical enquiry, consumers become passive readers of these visuals, unable to actively engage intellectually.

In examining popular historical memory, Raphael Samuel reminds readers how in the ancient world, pictorial art was of primary importance in learning and memory retention, "Something is not secure enough by hearing, but it is made firm by seeing."[18] Images not only remain fixed in one's memory in ways the written word does not, but they also reveal complexities and subtleties in their representations. John Berger made note of the significance of visuals by beginning the first chapter of his influential book *Ways of Seeing* by stating, "Seeing comes before words. The child looks and recognizes before it can speak."[19] In an increasing image-conscious world of Selfies, Instagram, and the Internet, visual language is acquired at a very young age; to ignore the significance of images, including cartoons and caricatures, can only be detrimental.

As political cartoons, these images have the potential to incite a strong emotional response that hinders the viewer from thinking critically. The examples of *Jyllands-Posten* "Muhammad" caricatures (2005), the *Charlie Hebdo* massacre (2015), and the *Herald Sun*'s Serena Williams caricature (2018), discussed in the Introduction raise important questions about freedom of speech and cultural sensitivities, geopolitical propaganda, the control over knowledge production and circulation, as well as the diverse ways of understanding and reacting to imagery. Political cartoons therefore became the focal points in a debate over "our" values versus "their" infraction; a resurgence of the same framework of discourse frequently utilised by *Punch* in the Victorian era. An intellectual and sensitive engagement with these visuals will only contribute to our understanding of the historical framework in which they were produced as well as their function. Additionally, the incorporation of political cartoons as serious scholarly source materials acknowledge the importance of visual thinking and ocular forms of information and knowledge formation, which directly affect how we understand and interact with the world and our surroundings.

Notes

1 "Mandarin Lo-Fun's Diary" *Punch*, Vol. 119 (28 November 1900), p. 379.
2 Esherick, *The Origins of the Boxer Uprising*, p. 311. Cohen, *History in Three Keys*, pp. 55–56.
3 Hevia, *English Lessons*, p. 319.
4 Timothy Brook, Jérôme Bourgon and Gregory Blue, *Death by a Thousand Cuts* (Cambridge, MA: Harvard University Press, 2008), p. 7.
5 Gregor Benton and Edmund Terence Gomez, *The Chinese in Britain, 1800-Present: Economy, Transnationalism, Identity* (Basingstoke: Palgrave Macmillan, 2008), p. 289.
6 This infamous drawing gave rise to various cartoons satirising the illustration for their own social or political commentary. One such depiction was from the Dutch artist Johann Braakensick who inverts the menacing Asian threat in "A New Interpretation of Kaiser Wilhelm's Picture." See Peter C. Perdue and Ellen Sebring, "The Boxer Uprising I: The Gathering Storm in North China, 1860–1900, Carving Up China" *MIT Visualizing Cultures*. Online: visualizingcultures.mit.edu/boxer_uprising/index.html.
7 Tobias Metzler, "We Must Prevent a Further Outbreak: Global Networks and the Fight Against the 'Yellow Peril'." Conference Paper given at *Transnational and Global History Seminar*, History Faculty, Oxford University, 13 June 2017.
8 David Walker, "Shooting Mabel: Warrior Masculinity and Asian Invasion" *History Australia*, Vol. 2, No. 3 (2005), 89.1–89.11.
9 Cited in Auerbach, *Race, Law, and 'The Chinese Puzzle' in Imperial Britain*, p. 1.
10 Auerbach, *Race, Law, and "The Chinese Puzzle" in Imperial Britain*, pp. 1–14.

11 W. J. T. Mitchell, *What Do Pictures Want?* (Chicago; London: University of Chicago Press, 2005), p. 297.
12 Witchard was referring specifically to *Aladdin* pantomimes. Witchard, *Thomas Burke's Dark "Chinoiserie,"* p. 61.
13 Christopher Frayling, *The Yellow Peril: Dr. Fu Manchu and the Rise of Chinaphobia* (London: Thames & Hudson, 2014), p. 9. His emphasis.
14 Curtis, Jr. *Apes and Angels*, p. IX.
15 Benton and Gomez, *The Chinese in Britain*, p. 288.
16 Ben Dowell, "Private Eye Hits Highest Circulation for More Than 25 Years" *The Guardian* (16 February 2012). Online: https://www.theguardian.com/media/2012/feb/16/private-eye-circulation-25-years.
17 John Jewell, "Private Eye Circulation Soars as Readers Turn to Satire – Funny, That. . ." *Independent* (15 February 2017). Online: https://www.independent.co.uk/arts-entertainment/private-eye-circulation-soars-as-readers-turn-to-satire-a7580826.html
18 Raphael Samuel, *Theatres of Memory: Past and Present in Contemporary Culture* (London; New York: Verso, 2012), p. XXI.
19 Berger, *Ways of Seeing*, p. 7.

BIBLIOGRAPHY

Periodical, diary, newspapers

BBC News, 2018.
Daily News
Evening Mail
The Examiner, 1848.
The Guardian, 2012–2017.
Illustrated London News

The Independent, 2017.
The Japan Gazette Office, 1879.
The New York Review of Books
The New York Times, 1895.
The North-China Herald
The North-China Herald (Shanghai)
The Pall Mall Gazette
Punch, 1841–1901.
The Spectator

The Times (London)

The Westminster Review

Primary and secondary sources

À Beckett, Arthur William. *The à Becketts of "Punch": Memories of Father and Sons.* New York: E.P. Dutton and Company, 1903.

Allan, James. *Under the Dragon Flag: My Experiences in the Chino-Japanese War.* London: W. Heinemann, 1898.

Allingham, Philip V. "George du Maurier, Illustrator and Novelist" *The Victorian Web: Literature, History and Culture in the Age of Victoria*. Online at www.victorianweb.org/art/illustration/dumaurier/pva95.html.

Altick, Richard D. *Punch: The Lively Youth of a British Institution, 1841–1851*. Columbus: Ohio State University, 1997.

Altick, Richard D. *The Shows of London*. Cambridge, MA: Belknap Press, 1978.

Appelbaum, Stanley and Richard Kelly (eds.). *Great Drawings and Illustrations From Punch, 1841–1901*. New York: Dover Publications, Inc., 1981.

Atkinson, Hoffman. *Exercises in the Yokohama Dialect*. Yokohama: The Japan Gazette Office, 1879.

Auerbach, Jeffrey. "The Great Exhibition and Historical Memory" *Journal of Victorian Culture*, Vol. 6, No. 1 (2001), pp. 89–112.

Auerbach, Jeffrey A. *The Great Exhibition of 1851: A Nation on Display*. New Haven, CT: Yale University Press, 1999.

Auerbach, Sascha. *Race, Law, and 'The Chinese Puzzle' in Imperial Britain*. New York: Palgrave Macmillan, 2009.

Banta, Martha. *Barbaric Intercourse: Caricature and the Culture of Conduct, 1841–1936*. Chicago; London: University of Chicago Press, 2003.

Behagg, Clive. *Labour and Reform: Working Class Movements 1815–1914*. London: Hodder and Stoughton, 1991.

Benjamin, Walter. *Illuminations*, translation by Harry Zohn. New York: Schocken, 1969.

Benton, Gregor and Edmund Terence Gomez. *The Chinese in Britain, 1800-Present: Economy, Transnationalism, Identity*. Basingstoke: Palgrave Macmillan, 2008.

Berger, John. *Ways of Seeing*. London: British Broadcasting Corporation in association with Penguin Books, 1972.

Berlioz, Hector. *Evenings with the Orchestra*, translated by Jacques Barzun. New York: Alfred A. Knopf, 1956.

Besant, Walter. *East London*. London: Chatto & Windus, 1901.

Bhabha, Homi K. "The Other Question: Stereotype, Discrimination and the Discourse of Colonialism" *The Location of Culture*. London: Routledge, 1994, pp. 66–84.

Bickers, Robert. *The Scramble for China: Foreign Devils in the Qing Empire, 1832–1914*. London: Allen Lane, 2011.

Blue, Gregory. "China and Western Social Thought in the Modern Period" *China and Historical Capitalism: Genealogies of Sinological Knowledge* (eds.) Timothy Brook and Gregory Blue. Cambridge: Cambridge University Press, 1999, pp. 57–109.

Booth, Martin. *Gweilo*. London: Bantham Books, 2005.

Brook, Timothy, Jérôme Bourgon and Gregory Blue. *Death by a Thousand Cuts*. Cambridge, MA: Harvard University Press, 2008.

Brown, David. "Diplomacy and the Fourth Estate: The Role of the Press in British Foreign Policy in the Age of Palmerston" *On the Fringes of Diplomacy: Influences on British Foreign Policy, 1800–1945* (eds.) John Fisher and Antony Best. Farnham; Burlington, VT: Ashgate Publishing Company, 2011, pp. 35–51.

Burke, Peter. *Eyewitnessing: The Uses of Images as Historical Evidence*. London: Reaktion Books Limited, 2001.

Burnand, Sir Frances C. *Records and Reminiscences, Personal and General*, Vol. II. London: Methuen & Co., 1904.

Burnett, John. *Plenty & Want: A Social History of Diet in England From 1815 to the Present Day*. London: Scolar Press, 1979.

Chaney, Michael A. "Heartfelt Thanks to Punch for the Picture: Frederick Douglass and the Transnational Jokework of Slave Caricature" *American Literature*, Vol. 82, No. 1 (March 2010), pp. 57–90.

Chang, Elizabeth Hope. *Britain's Chinese Eye: Literature, Empire, and Aesthetics in Nineteenth-Century Britain*. Stanford, CA: Stanford University Press, 2010.

Cheang, Sarah. "Selling China: Class, Gender and Orientalism at the Department Store" *Journal of Design History*, Vol. 20, No. 1 (Spring 2007), pp. 1–16.

Chen, Song-Chuan. *Merchants of War and Peace: British Knowledge of China in the Making of the Opium War*. Hong Kong: Hong Kong University Press, 2017.

Ciugureanu, Adina. "Mediating Between the Mass and the Individual: *Punch* Caricatures of the Great Exhibition of All Nations" *Gramma: Journal of Theory and Criticism*, Vol. 18 (2010), pp. 99–117.

Codell, Julie F. "Introduction" *Imperial Co-Histories: National Identities and the British and Colonial Press* (ed.) Julie F. Codell. Madison, NJ: Fairleigh Dickinson University Press; London: Associated University Presses, 2003, pp. 15–26.

Cody, Jeffrey W. and Frances Terpak (eds.). *Brush and Shutter: Early Photography in China*. Los Angeles, CA: Getty Research Institute, 2011.

Cohen, Michael. "Imagining Militarism: Art Young and *The Masses* Face the Enemy" *Radical History Review*, No. 106 (Winter 2010), pp. 87–108.

Cohen, Paul A. *History in Three Keys: The Boxers as Event, Experience, and Myth*. New York: Columbia University Press, 1997.

Cordery, Gareth. *An Edwardian's View of Dickens and His Illustrators: Harry Furniss's 'A Sketch of Boz'*. Greensboro: University of North Carolina, ELT Press, 2005.

Cordery, Gareth and Joseph Meisel (eds.). *The Humours of Parliament: Harry Furniss's View of Late-Victorian Political Culture*. Columbus: Ohio State University Press, 2014.

Crone, Rosalind. "Mr. and Mrs. Punch in Nineteenth-Century England" *The Historical Journal*, Vol. 49, No. 4 (December 2006), pp. 1055–1082.

Curtis, L. Perry, Jr. *Apes and Angels: The Irishman in Victorian Caricature*. Newton Abbot: David & Charles, Ltd., 1971.

Davis, John R. *The Great Exhibition*. Stroud: Sutton Publishing, 1999.

Day, Samuel Phillips. *Tea: Its Mystery and History*. London: Simpin, Marshall & Co., 1878.

Dibdin, Thomas. "Haul Away Boys" Bodleian Libraries, Harding B25 (812), Ballad – Roud Number V21062, Broadside Ballads. Online at ballads.bodleian.ox.ac.uk/view/sheet/4370.

Dingley, Robert and Richard Scully. "Courting the Colonies: Linley Sambourne, *Punch*, and Imperial Allegory" *Comic Empires: Imperialism in Cartoons, Caricature and Satirical Art* (eds.) Richard Scully and Andrekos Varnava. Manchester: Manchester University Press, 2019, pp. 31–65.

Diósy, Arthur. "The New Japan" *Japan as Seen and Described by Famous Writers*, edited and translated by Esther Singleton. New York: Dodd Mead and Co., 1904.

Dirlik, Arif. "Chinese History and the Question of Orientalism" *History and Theory*, Vol. 35, No. 4, Theme Issue 35: Chinese Historiography in Comparative Perspective (December 1996), pp. 96–118.

Donald, Diana. *The Age of Caricature: Satirical Prints in the Reign of George III*. New Haven; London: Yale University Press, 1996.

Dowell, Ben. "Private Eye Hits Highest Circulation for More Than 25 Years" *The Guardian*, 16 February 2012. Online at www.theguardian.com/media/2012/feb/16/private-eye-circulation-25-years.

Dower, John W. "Throwing off Asia II" *MIT Visualising Cultures*. Online at https://ocw.mit.edu/ans7870/21f/21f.027/throwing_off_asia_02/toa_essay01.html.

Du Maurier, George. *Social Pictorial Satire: Reminiscences and Appreciations of English Illustrators of the Past Generation*. New York; London: Harper & Brothers Publishers, 1898.

Dunn, Nathan and William B. Langdon. *"Ten Thousand Chinese Things": A Descriptive Catalogue of the Chinese*. London, England, 1843.

Dworkin, Ronald. "The Right to Ridicule" *The New York Review of Books*, 23 March 2006. Online at https://www.nybooks.com/articles/2006/03/23/the-right-to-ridicule.

Easley, Alexis, Andrew King and John Morton. "Introduction" *Researching the Nineteenth-Century Periodical Press: Case Studies* (eds.) Alexis Easley, Andrew King and John Morton. London: Routledge, Taylor & Francis Group, 2018, E-books online at the British Library.

Edwards, Steve. "The Accumulation of Knowledge or, William Whewell's Eye" *The Great Exhibition of 1851: New Interdisciplinary Essays* (ed.) Louise Purbick. Manchester; New York: Manchester University Press, 2001, pp. 26–52.

Ellis, Markman, Richard Coulton and Matthew Mauger. *Empire of Tea: The Asian Leaf That Conquered the World*. London: Reaktion Books Ltd., 2015.

Esherick, Joseph. *The Origins of the Boxer Uprising*. Berkeley; London: University of California Press, 1987.

Finnan, Joseph P. "Punch's Portrayal of Redmond, Carson and the Irish Question, 1910–18" *Irish Historical Studies*, Vol. 33, No. 132 (November 2003), pp. 424–445.

Forman, Ross G. *China and the Victorian Imagination: Empires Entwined*. Cambridge; New York: Cambridge University Press, 2013.

Forman, Ross G. "Peking Plots: Fictionalizing the Boxer Rebellion of 1900" *Victorian Literature and Culture*, Vol. 27, No. 1 (1999), pp. 19–48.

Fraser, Sarah E. "The Face of China: Photography's Role in Shaping Image, 1860–1920" *Getty Research Journal*, No. 2 (2010), pp. 39–52.

Frayling, Christopher. *The Yellow Peril: Dr. Fu Manchu and the Rise of Chinaphobia*. London: Thames & Hudson, 2014.

Frohlich, Judith. "Pictures of the Sino-Japanese War of 1894–1895" *War in History*, Vol. 21, No. 2 (2014), pp. 214–250.

Fromer, Julie E. *A Necessary Luxury: Tea in Victorian England*. Athens: Ohio University Press, 2008.

Godfrey, Leland Charles. "A New Dialect; or, Yokohama Pidgin" *New Quarterly Magazine*, London, Vol. 2 (July 1879), pp. 114–124.

Godley, Michael R. "The End of the Queue: Hair as Symbol in Chinese History" *China Heritage Quarterly*, The Australian National University, No. 27 (September 2011). Online at www.chinaheritagequarterly.org/features.php?searchterm=027_queue.inc&issue=027.

Graves, Charles L. *Mr. Punch's History of Modern England*, Vol. II: 1857–1874. London; New York; Toronto; Melbourne: Cassell and Company, Ltd., 1921.

Gray, Peter. "Punch and the Great Famine" *History Ireland*, Vol. 1, No. 2 (Summer 1993), pp. 26–33.

Gurney, Peter. "An Appropriated Space: The Great Exhibition, the Crystal Palace and the Working Class" *The Great Exhibition of 1851: New Interdisciplinary Essays* (ed.) Louise Purbick. Manchester; New York: Manchester University Press, 2001, pp. 114–145.

Habermas, Jürgen. *The Structural Transformation of the Public Sphere*, translated by Thomas Burger with the assistance of Frederick Lawrence. Cambridge: Polity Press, 1989.

Haddad, John R. "The Wild West Turns East: Audience, Ritual, and Regeneration in Buffalo Bill's Boxer Uprising" *American Studies*, Vol. 49, No. 3/4 (Fall/Winter 2008), pp. 5–38.

Harder, Hans. "Prologue: Late Nineteenth and Twentieth Century Asian Punch Versions and Related Satirical Journals" *Asian Punches, A Transcultural Affair* (eds.) Hans Harder and Barbara Mittler. Heidelberg: Springer, 2013, pp. 1–14.

Harris, Beth. "'Slaves of the Needle': The Seamstress in the 1840s" *The Victorian Web*, 14 December 2014. Online at http://www.victorianweb.org/gender/ugoretz1.html.

Hevia, James L. *Cherishing Men from Afar: Qing Guest Ritual and the Macartney Embassy of 1793*. Durham; London: Duke University Press, 1995.

Hevia, James L. *English Lessons: The Pedagogy of Imperialism in Nineteenth-century China*. Durham; Hong Kong: Duke University Press, 2003.

Hicks, Geoffrey. "Don Pacifico, Democracy, and Danger: The Protectionist Party Critique of British Foreign Policy, 1850–1852" *The International History Review*, Vol. 26, No. 3 (September 2004), pp. 515–540.

Howland, Douglas. "The Sinking of the S.S. Kowshing: International Law, Diplomacy, and the Sino-Japanese War" *Modern Asian Studies*, Vol. 42, No. 4 (July 2008), pp. 673–703.

Huggett, Frank E. *Victorian England as Seen by 'Punch'*. London: Book Club Associates, 1978.

Hugo, Victor. "Victor Hugo et le Sac du Palais D'Été" *Le Monde Diplomatique*, octobre 2004. Online at https://www.mode-diplomatique.fr/2004/10/HUGO/11563

Hung, Ho-Fung. "Orientalist Knowledge and Social Theories: China and the European Conceptions of East-West Differences from 1600 to 1900" *Sociological Theory*, Vol. 21, No. 3 (September 2003), pp. 254–280.

James, Henry. *Partial Portraits*. London: Macmillan and Co., 1888.

James, Henry. *The Painter's Eye: Notes and Essays on the Pictorial Arts*, edited by John L. Sweeney. London: Rupert Hart-Davis, 1956.

Janes, Dominic. "The Role of Visual Appearance in Punch's Early Victorian Satires on Religion" *Victorian Periodicals Review*, Vol. 47, No. 1 (Spring 2014), pp. 66–86.

Jerrold, Walter. *Douglas Jerrold and 'Punch'*. London: Macmillan and Co., Limited, 1910.

Jerrold, William Blanchard. *The Life and Remains of Douglas Jerrold: By His Son, Blanchard Jerrold*. Boston: Ticknor and Fields, 1859.

Jerrold, William Blanchard. *The Wit and Opinions of Douglas Jerrold*. London: Winchester, 1859.

Jewell, John. "Private Eye Circulation Soars as Readers Turn to Satire – Funny, That. . ." *Independent*, 15 February 2017. Online at www.independent.co.uk/arts-entertainment/private-eye-circulation-soars-as-readers-turn-to-satire-a7580826.html.

Jordan, H. Donaldson. "The Case of Richard Cobden" *Proceedings of the Massachusetts Historical Society*, Third Series, Vol. 83 (1971), pp. 34–45.

Kent, Christopher. "War Cartooned/Cartoon War: Matt Morgan and the American Civil War in 'Fun' and 'Frank Leslie's Illustrated Newspaper'" *Victorian Periodicals Review*, Vol. 36, No. 2 (Summer 2003), pp. 153–181.

Kersten, Holger. "America's Multilingualism and the Problem of the Literary Representation of 'Pidgin English.'" *Amerikastudien/American Studies*, Vol. 51, No. 1, Multilingualism and American Studies (2006), pp. 75–91.

Klausen, Jytte. *The Cartoons That Shook the World*. New Haven: Yale University Press, 2009.

Layard, George Somes. *Shirley Brooks of Punch, His Life, Letters, and Diaries.* New York: Henry Holt and Company, 1907.

Layard, George Somes. *The Life and Letters of Charles Samuel Keene of 'Punch'*. London: Sampson Low, Marston & Company, Limited, 1893.

Leary, Patrick. *The Punch Brotherhood: Table Talk and Print Culture in Mid-Victorian London*. London: The British Library, 2010.

Levin, Michael. *J.S. Mill on Civilization and Barbarism*. London: Routledge, 2004.

Li, Michelle, Stephen Matthews and Geoff P. Smith. "Pidgin English Texts from the Chinese English Instructor" *Chinese Pidgin English: Texts and Contexts* (eds.) Geoff P. Smith and Stephen Matthews, The English Centre; The University of Hong Kong, Vol. 10, No. 1 (September 2005), pp. 79–167.

Liu, Lydia H. "The Thug, the Barbarian, and the Work of Imperial Warfare" *Modern Language Association*, Vol. 124, No. 5 (October 2009), pp. 1859–1863.

Lovell, Julia. *The Opium War.* London: Picador, 2011.

Maidment, Brian. "Pencillings, Cuts and Cartoons: *Punch* and Early Victorian Comic Illustration" *Punch Historical Archive 1841–1992*. Cengage Learning, 2014.

Maidment, Brian. "The Presence of *Punch* in the Nineteenth Century" *Asian Punches, a Transcultural Affair* (eds.) Hans Harder and Barbara Mittler. Heidelberg: Springer, 2013.

Mantell, Gideon. *The Journal of Gideon Mantell*, edited by E. Cecil Curwen. London: Oxford University Press, 1940.

Martin, Basil Kingsley. *The Triumph of Lord Palmerston: A Study of Public Opinion in England Before the Crimean War.* London: G. Allen & Unwin, 1924.

Matthews, Stephen. Personal Notes. University of Hong Kong, 19 December 2016.

Matthewson, Amy. "Satirising Imperial Anxiety in Victorian Britain: Representing Japan in *Punch* Magazine, 1852–1893" *Contemporary Japan* (2021), pp. 1–24.

Maurer, Oscar. "'Punch' on Slavery and Civil War in America" *Victorian Studies*, Vol. 1, No. 1 (September 1957), pp. 4–28.

May, J. P. "The Chinese in Britain, 1860–1914" *Immigrants and Minorities in British Society* (ed.) Colin Holmes. London: Allen and Unwin, 1978, pp. 111–124.

Mayhew, Athol. *A Jorum of 'Punch'*. London: Downey & Co., 1895.

Mayhew, Henry. *London Labour & the London Poor*, edited by Robert Douglas-Fairhurst. Oxford: Oxford University Press, 2010.

McLean, D. "The Foreign Office and the First Chinese Indemnity Loan, 1895" *The Historical Journal*, Vol. 16, No. 2 (June 1973), pp. 303–321.

McNees, Eleanor. "'Punch' and the Pope: Three Decades of Anti-Catholic Caricature" *Victorian Periodicals Review*, Vol. 37, No. 1 (Spring 2004), pp. 18–45.

Message, Kylie and Ewan Johnston. "The World Within the City: The Great Exhibition, Race, Class and Social Reform" *Britain, the Empire, and the World at the Great Exhibition of 1851* (eds.) Jeffrey A. Auerback and Peter H. Hoffenberg. Burlington, VT: Ashgate, 2008, pp. 27–46.

Metzler, Tobias. "We Must Prevent a Further Outbreak: Global Networks and the Fight Against the 'Yellow Peril'" Conference Paper given at *Transnational and Global History Seminar*, History Faculty, Oxford University, 13 June 2017.

Millar, J. H. "The Life of 'Punch'" *Blackwood's Edinburgh Magazine*, December 1895, pp. 866–879.

Miller, Henry. "The Problem with Punch" *Institute of Historical Research*, Vol. 82, No. 216 (May 2009), pp. 285–302.

Miller, Henry J. "John Leech and the Shaping of the Victorian Cartoon: The Context of Respectability" *Victorian Periodicals Review*, Vol. 42, No. 3 (Fall 2009), pp. 267–291.

Mitchell, W. J. T. *What Do Pictures Want?* Chicago; London: University of Chicago Press, 2005.

Morris, Frankie. *Artist of Wonderland: The Life, Political Cartoons, and Illustrations of Tenniel.* Cambridge: The Lutterworth Press, 2005.

Murawska-Muthesius, Katarzyna. "On Small Nations and Bullied Children: Mr. Punch Draws Eastern Europe" *The Slavonic and East European Review*, Vol. 84, No. 2 (April 2006), pp. 279–305.

Navasky, Victor S. *The Art of Controversy: Political Cartoons and their Enduring Power.* New York: Alfred A. Knopf, 2013.

Nish, Ian. "Politics, Trade and Communications in East Asia: Thoughts on Anglo-Russian Relations, 1861–1907" *Modern Asian Studies*, Vol. 21, No. 4 (1987), pp. 667–678.

Ormond, Leonée. "Edward Linley Sambourne: A Cartoonist in the Art World" *The British Art Journal*, Vol. 3, No. 1 (Autumn 2001), pp. 5–11.

Orwell, George. *Burmese Days*. London: Penguin in association with Martin Secker and Warburg, 1989.

Otte, T. G. "'Avenge England's Dishonour': By-Elections, Parliament and the Politics of Foreign Policy in 1898" *The English Historical Review*, Vol. 121, No. 491 (April 2006), pp. 385–428.

Otte, T. G. *The China Question: Great Power Rivalry and British Isolation, 1894–1905*. New York: Oxford University Press, 2007.

Pagani, Catherine. "Chinese Material Culture and British Perceptions of China in the Mid-Nineteenth Century" *Colonialism and the Object: Empire, Material Culture and the Museum* (eds.) Tim Barringer and Tom Flynn. London: Routledge, 1998, pp. 28–40.

Pagani, Catherine. "Objects and the Press: Images of China in Nineteenth-Century Britain" *Imperial Co-Histories* (ed.) Julie F. Codell. Madison, NJ: Fairleigh Dickinson University Press; London: Associated University Presses, 2003, pp. 147–166.

Paine, S. C. M. *The Sino-Japanese War of 1894–1895*. Cambridge; New York: Cambridge University Press, 2003.

Pearson, Richard. "Thackeray and *Punch* at the Great Exhibition: Authority and Ambivalence in Verbal and Visual Caricatures" *The Great Exhibition of 1851: New Interdisciplinary Essays* (ed.) Louise Purbick. Manchester; New York: Manchester University Press, 2001, pp. 179–205.

Perdue, Peter C. and Ellen Sebring. "The Boxer Uprising: The Gathering Storm in North China, 1860–1900" *Massachusetts Institute of Technology, Visualizing Cultures* (2016). Online at visualizingcultures.mit.edu/boxer_uprising/index.html.

Peters, Diane. "A Celebration of Empire: Queen Victoria's Diamond Jubilee" *CAML Review/Revue de L'ACBM*, Vol. 26, No. 2 (1998), pp. 25–29.

Polachek, James M. *The Inner Opium War*. Cambridge, MA; London: Harvard University, Council on East Asian Studies, 1992.

Potter, Simon J. "Communication and Integration: The British and Dominions Press and the British World, c.1876–1914" *The Journal of Imperial and Commonwealth History*, Vol. 31, No. 2 (2003), pp. 190–206.

PUNCH Magazine Cartoon Archive. Online at http://www.punch.co.uk/about/.

Purbrick, Louise. "Introduction" *The Great Exhibition of 1851: New Interdisciplinary Essays* (ed.) Louise Purbick. Manchester; New York: Manchester University Press, 2001, pp. 1–25.

Rappaport, Erika. *A Thirst for Empire: How Tea Shaped the Modern World*. Princeton, NJ: Princeton University Press, 2017.

Rappaport, Erika. "Object Lessons and Colonial Histories: Inventing the Jubilee of Indian Tea" BRANCH: *Britain, Representation and Nineteenth-Century History* (ed.) Dino Franco Felluga. Extension of *Romanticism and Victorianism on the Net*. Online at http://www.branchcollective.org/?ps_articles=erika-rappaport-object-lessons-and-colonial-histories-inventing-the-jubilee-of-indian-tea.

Reeve, Alan and Martin Reeve. "Punch and Judy at the Beach and in the Mall" *Visual Culture in Britain*, Vol. 12, No. 1 (2011), pp. 17–31.

Reynolds, Diana J. "The Great Exhibition of 1851 – Interpretive Essay" *Events That Changed Great Britain Since 1689* (eds.) Frank W. Thackeray and John E. Findling, Westport, CT; London: Greenwood, 2002, pp. 98–111.

Ricalton, James. *China Through the Stereoscope; a Journey Through the Dragon Empire at the Time of the Boxer Uprising*. New York: Underwood & Underwood, 1901.

Richter, Virginia. "Laughter and Aggression: Desire and Derision in a Postcolonial Context" *Cheeky Fictions: Laughter and the Postcolonial* (eds.) Susanne Reichl and Mark Stein. Amsterdam; New York: Rodopi, 2005, pp. 61–72.

Ruskin, John. *The Art of England: Lectures Given in Oxford.* New York: J. Wiley & Sons, 1884.

Said, Edward. *Orientalism.* New York: Vintage Books, 1979.

Sambourne, Edward Linley. Diary. Royal Borough of Kensington and Chelsea. Leighton House, Sambourne House. Online at www.issuu.com/leighton-house_sambourne-house/stacks/5fa0d3ebff634c49a95117ffbe20c7ee

Samuel, Raphael. *Theatres of Memory: Past and Present in Contemporary Culture.* London; New York: Verso, 2012.

Scully, Richard. "A Pettish Little Emperor" *Drawing the Line: Using Cartoons as Historical Evidence* (eds.) Richard Scully and Marian Quartly. Clayton, Victoria: Monash University ePress, 2009. Online at http://books.publishing.monash.edu.

Scully, Richard. *British Images of Germany: Admiration, Antagonism & Ambivalence, 1860–1914.* Basingstoke: Palgrave Macmillan, 2012.

Scully, Richard. "Constructing the Colossus: The Origins of Linley Sambourne's Greatest 'Punch' Cartoon" *International Journal of Comic Art*, Vol. 14, No. 2 (2012), pp. 120–142.

Scully, Richard and Marian Quartly. "Using Cartoons as Historical Evidence" *Drawing the Line: Using Cartoons as Historical Evidence* (eds.) Richard Scully and Marian Quartly. Clayton, Victoria: Monash University ePress, 2009. Online at http://books.publishing.monash.edu. (Accessed 11 May 2018).

Scully, Richard and Andrekos Varnava. "Introduction: The Importance of Cartoons, Caricature, and Satirical Art in Imperial Contexts" *Comic Empires: Imperialism in Cartoons, Caricature and Satirical Art* (eds.) Richard Scully and Andrekos Varnava. Manchester: Manchester University Press, 2019, pp. 1–27.

Short, Audrey. "Workers Under Glass in 1851" *Victorian Studies*, Vol. 10, No. 2 (December 1966), pp. 193–202.

Silver, Henry. Diary. *Punch* Archive. British Library.

Simpson, Roger. "King Arthur at the 'Punch' Round Table, 1859–1914" *Arthuriana*, Vol. 9, No. 4 (Winter 1999), pp. 94–115.

Simpson, Roger. *Sir John Tenniel: Aspects of His Work.* London: Associated University Presses, 1994.

Spielmann, M. H. *The History of 'Punch'.* London: Cassell & Company, Limited, 1895.

Spinks, Charles Nelson. "The Background of the Anglo-Japanese Alliance" *Pacific Historical Review*, Vol. 8, No. 3 (September 1939), pp. 317–339.

Spurr, David. *The Rhetoric of Empire: Colonial Discourse in Journalism, Travel Writing, and Imperial Administration.* Durham; London: Duke University Press, 1993.

Stenz, Georg Maria. *Life of Father Richard Henle, S.V.D.: Missionary in China: Assassinated November 1, 1897.* Techny, IL: Mission Press, S.V.D., 1915.

Suleman, Reena. "Out of the Ordinary: Linley Sambourne and the Amateur Model" *The British Art Journal*, Vol. 3, No. 1 (Autumn 2001), pp. 28–35.

Tallis, John. *Tallis's History and Description of the Crystal Palace, and the Exhibition of the World's Industry in 1851.* London; New York: J. Tallis and Co., 1851, Vol. 1 & 2.

Taylor, Miles. "John Bull and the Iconography of Public Opinion in England c. 1712–1929" *Past & Present*, No. 134 (February 1992), pp. 93–128.

"The Chinese War" *The Comic Album: A Book for Every Table.* London: Orr and Co., 1842. *The Curran Index* (eds.) Lara Atkin and Emily Bell. 2017-present. Online at curranindex.org.

Tong, Q. S. "Traveling Imperialism: Lord Elgin's Missions to China and the Limits of Victorian Liberalism" *A Century of Travels in China* (eds.) Douglas Kerr and Julia Kuehn. Hong Kong: Hong Kong University Press, 2007, pp. 39–52.

Töpffer, Rodolphe. De la plaque Daguerre: À propos des Excursions daguerriennes. Cognac: Le temps qu'il fait, 2002.

Twain, Mark. *The Mysterious Stranger and Other Stories.* New York; London: Harper & Brothers Publishers, 1922.

Tythacott, Louise. *The Lives of Chinese Objects.* New York: Berghahn Books, 2011.

Van Dijk, Kees. *Pacific Strife: The Great Powers and Their Political and Economic Rivalries in Asia and the Western Pacific 1870–1914.* Amsterdam: Amsterdam University Press, 2015.

Vanke, Francesca. "Degrees of Otherness: The Ottoman Empire and China at the Great Exhibition of 1851" *Britain, the Empire, and the World at the Great Exhibition of 1851* (eds.) Jeffrey A. Auerbach and Peter H. Hoffenberg. Aldershot, England; Burlington, VT: Ashgate Publishing Ltd., 2008, pp. 191–205.

Villiers, Frederick. "The Truth About Port Arthur" *The North American Review*, Vol. 160, No. 460 (March 1895), pp. 327–328.

Vorachek, Laura. "Mesmerists and Other Meddlers: Social Darwinism, Degeneration, and Eugenics in Trilby" *Victorian Literature and Culture*, Vol. 37, No. 1 (2009), pp. 197–215.

Wagner, Rudolf G. "China 'Asleep' and 'Awakening': A Study in Conceptualizing Asymmetry and Coping with It" *Transcultural Studies*, No. 1 (2011), pp. 4–139.

Walker, David. "Shooting Mabel: Warrior Masculinity and Asian Invasion" *History Australia*, Vol. 2, No. 3 (2005), 89.1–89.11.

Waller, Philip. "Roman Candles: Catholic Converts Among Authors in Late-Victorian and Edwardian Britain" *Politics and Culture in Victorian Britain* (eds.) Peter Ghosh and Lawrence Goldman. Oxford; New York: Oxford University Press, 2006, pp. 192–219.

West, Shearer. "Tom Taylor, William Powell Frith, and the British School of Art" *Victorian Studies*, Vol. 33, No. 2 (Winter 1990), pp. 307–326.

White, E. B. "Some Remarks on Humor" *In the Words of E.B. White: Quotations from America's Most Companionable of Writers* (ed.) Martha White. Ithaca: Cornell University Press, 2011.

Williams, Dominic. "*Punch* and the Pogroms: Eastern Atrocities in John Tenniel's Political Cartoons, 1876–1896" *RACAR: Revue d'art Canadienne/Canadian Art Review*, Vol. 42, No. 1 (2017), pp. 32–47.

Witchard, Anne Veronica. *Thomas Burke's Dark 'Chinoiserie': Limehouse Nights and the Queer Spell of Chinatown.* Farnham, UK: Ashgate Publishing Limited, 2009.

Wong, J. Y. *Deadly Dreams: Opium, Imperialism and the 'Arrow' War (1856–60) in China.* Cambridge: Cambridge University Press, 1998.

Yates, Edmund. "His Recollections and Experiences: Victorian London – Entertainment and Recreation – Museums, Public Buildings and Galleries – The Chinese Collection/Chinese Exhibition" *The Victorian Dictionary: Exploring Victorian London* (ed.) Lee Jackson. Online at www.victorianlondon.org/entertainment/chinesecollection.htm.

Young, Paul. "Mission Impossible: Globalization and the Great Exhibition" *Britain, the Empire, and the World at the Great Exhibition of 1851* (eds.) Jeffrey A. Auerbach and Peter H. Hoffenberg. London; New York: Ashgate Publishing, 2008, pp. 3–26.

Zhang Zhenjian. *Language and Society in Early Hong Kong, 1841–1884*, unpublished Ph.D. Dissertation. University of Hong Kong.

Ziter, Edward. *The Orient on the Victorian Stage.* Cambridge: Cambridge University Press, 2003.

INDEX

Page numbers for *tables* and *figures* are represented by **bolds** and *italics* respectively.

For Product Safety Concerns and Information please contact our EU representative GPSR@taylorandfrancis.com
Taylor & Francis Verlag GmbH, Kaufingerstraße 24, 80331 München, Germany

www.ingramcontent.com/pod-product-compliance
Lightning Source LLC
Chambersburg PA
CBHW071116100726
47908CB00008B/2390

* 9 7 8 0 3 6 7 4 6 0 9 9 0 *